1 BEGINNINGS OF EMPIRE

Hannibal invades Italy

African elephants on Carthaginian coins. They are larger and heavier than Indian elephants, but more difficult to train and control.

Imagine an army marching along the Mediterranean coast of Spain. Foot-soldiers from many countries, speaking different languages and with all kinds of weapons and armour are strung out in a dusty column. Numidian horsemen from the desert fringes of North Africa ride beside and ahead of the marching infantry. They scout the route and protect the flanks. Elephants plod along with trunks swinging, while thousands of pack animals carry all the equipment and haul the heavy wagons. This is the army of the Carthaginian general Hannibal as he begins his march from Spain towards Italy. There he plans to make war on Rome and destroy her power, so that Carthage will once again rule the Western Mediterranean.

SOURCE 1A

They got the elephants across like this. First they built a heavy pier of rafts, jutting into the river with a separate double-raft loosely attached to the far end. Next they piled earth along the pier to make it look like a path leading down to the river crossing. They drove the elephants, with two females leading, along the raft pier. As soon as they were standing on the double-raft at the end, the ropes were cut and the boats pulled the raft, with the elephants standing on it, out into mid-stream. At first the animals panicked, but when they saw water all round, they were so afraid that they stayed quiet, and so crossed safely. Later, some elephants were so terrified that they leaped into the river when they were only half-way across. Their drivers were drowned, but the elephants were saved because of the power and length of their trunks, which they kept above the surface. They could breathe through these, and spout out any water which entered their mouths. In this way, most of them survived.

Hannibal: a portrait on a coin made in Spain.

Look at the map on page 2. To reach Italy, 1,500 miles away, Hannibal had to cross the Pyrenees, the wide river Rhone and finally the Alps, the highest mountain barrier in Europe. No wonder the soldiers sometimes wanted to turn back. Source 1A tells how the historian Polybius describes the crossing of the Rhone:

The struggle through the Alps

Hannibal then turned his army towards the last and greatest obstacle before Italy, the Alps. Here he faced two enemies, dangerous mountain passes and hostile hill-tribes. Many men and animals died, but at last the exhausted army reached the top of the pass. 'Soldiers', said Hannibal, 'you have now climbed the walls of Italy and of Rome itself. From now on the going is easy, and downhill!'

INVESTIGATIONS

How Hannibal won his victories
What sort of people the Romans were
How the Romans governed themselves
How they controlled Italy

Key sources
● Ancient writers
● Archaeological finds and remains
● Statues, carvings and coins

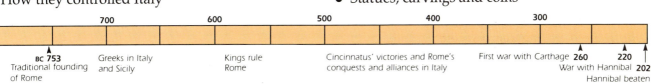

700	600	500	400	300

BC 753
Traditional founding of Rome

Greeks in Italy and Sicily

Kings rule Rome

Cincinnatus' victories and Rome's conquests and alliances in Italy

First war with Carthage 260

220

War with Hannibal 202
Hannibal beaten

But the way down, although shorter, was steeper and more treacherous. The historian, Livy, describes the terrible downward march:

SOURCE 1B

They could not grip the slippery ice and there were no stumps or roots to hold on to. All they could do was slither down. . . . A huge rock blocked the path, so they cut down some trees and built a bonfire round it. When it was hot, the soldiers threw their rations of sour wine onto it, to make it crack. Finally, they split the boulder with picks and hammers and so cleared the path.

Five months after leaving Spain, Hannibal's army reached the green plains of north Italy, 'ghosts and shadows of men' as the Roman commander called them. Since crossing the Rhone, Hannibal had lost 36,000 men and many pack-animals and elephants. Rome's defending legions were marching quickly to face him.

1.1 What kind of commander has Hannibal shown himself to be so far?　AT 1.4

1.2 Imagine that you are one of Hannibal's soldiers. Write down your feelings about the march and the months ahead. Use a modern atlas to work out how far you have marched since leaving Sagunto (near Valencia) in Spain.　AT 1.6

Historians

This chapter contains quotations from two historians who wrote in ancient times.

Titus Livius (Livy) 59 BC–AD 17, wrote a 142-volume history of Rome from its earliest days to his own times. He certainly brought the past to life and succeeded in his main aim – to show how Rome rose to greatness, despite the setbacks.

Polybius 200–118 BC, was a Greek, taken to Rome in 168 BC as a political prisoner. He became friendly with many important Romans, and re-traced Hannibal's route through the Alps.

1.3 Which of these two historians is likely to write the more trustworthy account of the war with Hannibal? Why?　AT 3.6

1.4 What are the advantages and drawbacks of writing a history soon after the events have taken place?　AT 2.7

1.5 Why is it difficult to describe a journey in a way which can be followed centuries later?　AT 1.4

The land of Italy

The Alps have always been a major barrier to anyone invading Italy from the north. The passes are usually clear of snow from May to September, but any attacking army had a long climb to about 2,000 metres followed by a steep descent to the river Po. The mountains are also 150 miles wide in places, so armies from the north rarely threatened Rome and Italy. As Hannibal looked back up at the towering peaks of the Alps from the plains he must have thought that he had overcome the most difficult obstacle.

1.6 Hannibal crossed the Alps in autumn. What risks was he running?　AT 1.4

1.7 Hannibal's elephants caused many problems during his march through the mountains. Why do you think he brought them?　AT 1.4

South of the Alps, the plains where Hannibal and his army spent the winter were inhabited by tribes of Gauls. It was almost two centuries before this fertile area became part of 'Italia'. Further south,

SOURCE 1C　**Italy, showing the high ground, main rivers and the regions and cities mentioned in this chapter.**

INTRODUCTION

The Mediterranean and its kingdoms

The place where Rome now stands was once just a convenient crossing-place on the river Tiber in western Italy. Long before the first tiny settlement appeared, many different peoples and kingdoms were spread along the Mediterranean coasts. The map shows who they were, where they lived and when they were most powerful.

'We have settled on the shores of this sea like frogs round a pond,' wrote one famous Greek philosopher. And he was right. Some of the world's earliest civilisations sprang up around the Mediterranean. You have probably studied the Egyptians and read stories of the kingdom of Israel in the Old Testament. While the first Romans were building their small settlement, about 800 BC, Greek and Phoenician sailors were already exploring new lands and starting colonies around the Mediterranean. They took their way of life, languages and beliefs with them, to the Black Sea coast and the Straits of Gibraltar, Spain and the south of France. When Alexander the Great defeated the Persians and took over their lands, by 323 BC, the year of his death, his Greek empire stretched from Libya in the west to the boundaries of India in the east.

Our story begins in the western Mediterranean, about 100 years after the death of Alexander. Two cities, Rome and Carthage, were rivals for power. Roman armies had already won one war and seized some Carthaginian lands. But Carthage was determined to fight back, and her brilliant young general, Hannibal, collected a powerful new army in Spain.

You will soon find out what happened to Hannibal and to the Roman armies who faced him. You will also discover how Rome, the city on the Tiber

- gained control of all the lands around the Mediterranean

- became the centre of a great empire

- brought its way of life to millions of people and

- helped to spread the ideas, beliefs and achievements of the Mediterranean civilisations through Europe and the world.

Q Why would Carthage and Rome be in a good position to dominate the Mediterranean?

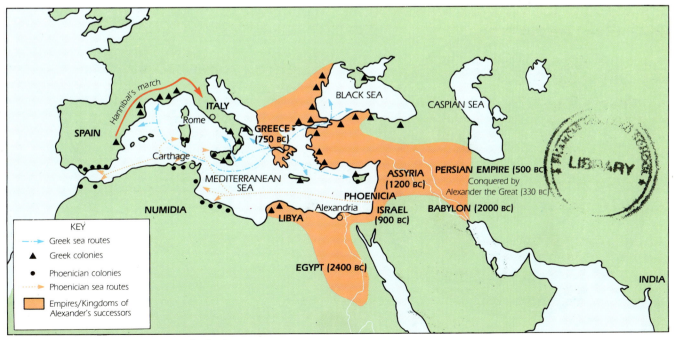

The Mediterranean Sea. Its name in Latin means 'The sea in the middle of the lands'. It is over 3000 km long.

How to use this book

When we study history, we try to discover what happened in the past and why. This can be exciting and sometimes puzzling.

Evidence

We use evidence from sources (pictures, objects or writing) which come from the time in the past which we are studying. As we do this we must ask questions about the source:

- Who wrote it or produced it?

- Can we find out its date, and where it comes from?

- What definite information does it give us?

- Can we make any sensible guesses from the information it gives?

- What does it *not* tell us?

A written source may be biased but is still useful. It tells us the feelings of the person who wrote it, and what he or she thought was important. When written sources leave something out, there may be a reason for that too. Those in this book were written in Latin or Greek: they have been translated into English and sometimes made simpler and shorter.

Primary evidence comes from sources produced at the time, like Hadrian's Wall, Julius Caesar's descriptions of the wars he himself fought, coins or inscriptions on buildings or tombstones.

Secondary evidence comes from ancient writers describing times even earlier than their own, like Livy's history of early Rome.

Questions

These make you think about what you have read or seen, and help you to understand it.

Pointers

Signs like this ◁▭ point you to earlier or later pages, and help you to link up and remember what you have read.

Glossary and index

This explains important words which may be difficult or unfamiliar, and refers you to the right page in the text.

Emperor Vespasian – a coin portrait.

Graffiti portrait from a wall in Pompeii.

Hannibal could see another range of mountains, the Apennines, separating the northern plain from the peninsula of Italy. They form the 'backbone' of Italy. Although not as high as the Alps, the passes can be difficult in winter. The Apennines had many well-fortified towns in their foot-hills. Some of these can be seen today, their walls still standing. The mountains also tend to divide Italy into two coastal strips [See 1C]. The eastern strip is narrower and less fertile and lacks natural harbours, except in the south. In the west lay the most fertile areas of ancient Italy – the plains of Campania around Naples and Latium around Rome, and the hill-slopes of Etruria further north. Much of the soil of the western region is rich and volcanic. The two main western rivers, the Tiber and the Arno, were deep enough for sailing vessels in ancient times. Because the west had these advantages, more people lived there, and they played a more important part in the history of Italy.

Orvieto, an Italian hill-town. Notice its position.

This is how one writer, Pliny the Elder, described the land and climate in his Encyclopaedia of Natural History:

SOURCE 1D

The land is blessed by its position between the east and the west Mediterranean, its healthy, temperate climate, its easy access to foreign lands, its many-harboured coasts and favourable winds. . . . Then there are her plentiful waters, cooling woodlands, mountain passes, unaggressive wild animals, fertile soil and rich pasture. No other land produces better cereals, wine, olive oil, wool, flax, clothing or cattle; and in mining for gold, silver, copper and iron, Italy is second to none.

1.8 Which details of Pliny's description seem exaggerated? Compare his views with what you can find out about ancient and modern Italy. **[AT 3.6]**

1.9 What do you think is particularly fortunate about Italy's position 'between the east and the west'? How long a journey was it from Sicily to North Africa and from southern Italy to Greece? **[AT 3.3]**

1.10 Does the geography of a country affect its history and what happens there? Find as many examples as you can to prove either that it does, or that it does not. **[AT 1.4]**

The countryside in Italy today. Notice the crops.

Hannibal's victories

When the Roman and the Carthaginian armies met in battle, Hannibal soon proved himself a brilliant general. He used all his troops skilfully, particularly the cavalry, and got to know the character and weaknesses of his Roman enemies. Soon he was marching south towards central Italy. There, on the shores of Lake Trasimene, he lured a Roman army into an ambush, and trapped them between the mountains and the lake. This is Livy's description of how the Roman soldiers felt when Hannibal's men sprang their surprise attack:

SOURCE 1E

They knew they were surrounded: the enemy battle-cry came from all sides. In the confusion, no-one knew his proper place in the ranks. As the mist rolled round them, they were guided by their ears, not their eyes. They turned to face every sound – the groans of wounded men, the thud of blows on bodies or shields, the attackers' shouts, the cries of fear. Some, as they fled, crashed into groups who were still holding their ground: others, trying to return to the fight, were forced back by those who were running away.

A new war-plan for Rome

These soldiers were carved on ivory in the years before the war with Hannibal.

City walls of Perugia, in central Italy. The massive stone blocks in the lower part of the picture were there when Hannibal marched past on his way to Lake Trasimene. He did not try to capture the city.

More than 15,000 Romans died that day. When news reached Rome, the Senate feared that Hannibal would now attack Rome itself. So they appointed a supreme commander, whom Romans called a *'dictator'*, to strengthen the city's walls and destroy the bridges. But he did more. First, he ordered the people to perform all the correct religious ceremonies and offer public prayers – for the gods were obviously very angry. Then he proposed a new way of fighting Hannibal: the Roman army should avoid battle. Instead they should follow Hannibal at a distance, attacking only small groups when they were separated from his main army. This 'delaying' strategy later proved very successful, but many Romans thought it was cowardly to refuse to fight. So they recruited another army, and Hannibal had another chance to show that he was a much better general than any Roman. At the battle of Cannae, in 216 BC, he completely destroyed the new Roman army: more than 50,000 Romans were killed. Even Hannibal's own men were shocked at the sight when they came back to the battlefield next day to collect their booty. Livy describes the scene:

SOURCE 1F

All over the battlefield Roman soldiers lay dead, in their thousands, cavalry and foot-soldiers together. Here and there wounded men, covered in blood, revived by the morning cold, were cut down as they struggled out from among the corpses. Some had their knee or thigh ligaments sliced through: they bared their throats, and begged Hannibal's men to spill the little blood they had left. Some had their heads buried in the ground; they had dug themselves holes, and by smothering their faces with earth had choked themselves to death.

1.11 How does Livy make these dreadful battle-scenes seem so vivid? `AT 2.7`

1.12 Livy was writing 200 years later. Where would he find detailed information about the battles he described? May he have invented some incidents? If so, why? `AT 3.7`

1.13 What important lesson did the defeat at Cannae teach the Romans? `AT 3.4`

1.14 Imagine that you are a senator and an experienced soldier. Make a speech to the senate, telling them how dangerous Hannibal is, and how you think he can be beaten. `AT 1.4`

The turning-point

Hannibal now thought about marching on Rome. But he knew that a siege would be long and difficult. Instead he tried to persuade Rome's allies throughout Italy to break their treaties, or agreements, with Rome. If this happened, Hannibal believed, Rome would lose her power and Carthage would once again control the western Mediterranean.

Italian warriors carry their dead comrade from the battlefield. This group of figures forms the handle of a bronze lid.

But Rome refused to give in. As the years went by, some supporters did desert her, but most remained loyal. Rome's generals now used the 'delaying' tactics and were not drawn into battles, so time was on Rome's side. Every year, new troops were trained and new armies recruited. Roman commanders were sent overseas to attack Carthaginian territory in Spain and Sicily. They prevented reinforcements from reaching Hannibal. So he was isolated, far from home and had no chance to win another battle in Italy.

Reasons for Roman success

How were the Romans able to fight back so well? There is no simple answer to questions like this, but most writers in ancient times and today believe that there were several reasons for Rome's success. We shall look at some of the most important ones:

1 The character of the Roman people

2 Their belief in the gods and Rome's destiny

3 The strength of the Roman family and of the government

4 Roman manpower and military discipline

5 The way Rome treated the other peoples and cities in Italy.

Roman Character

When we talk about a 'typical' Roman, or Frenchman or Scot, we are often being unfair. But Romans like Livy believed that their ancestors had a special 'Roman' character called 'our ancestors' way of life', and were sure that it had helped them to beat Hannibal and other enemies. For Romans, this 'ancestral way of life' meant a tough existence. They had to work hard on their tiny farms outside the city, defending their lands and always being loyal, determined and brave in peace and war. As we look back at Rome's earliest years we can agree that the citizens of early Rome owed their success to their strong character. For more than five centuries they had worked and fought on the western plains, beating off the raiding hill-tribes. Their city was seized by nearby tribes, then destroyed by the Gauls. But the Romans never gave up, and gradually won control of most of Italy. Ancient writers liked to retell the stories of their ancestors' victories, and to describe the simple lives of the early farmer-soldiers. Livy tells how a dictator was needed to deal with a crisis when a Roman army had been ambushed:

SOURCE 1G

Lucius Cincinnatus was the people's only hope. He was cultivating his farm – just three acres, on the west side of the Tiber. The senate's messengers found him digging ditches, or at any rate working on his land. They greeted each other, and then the messengers asked him to put on his toga and listen to the senate's orders. 'What's wrong?' he asked in surprise, and told his wife Racilia to run and get his toga from their cottage. Next, wiping off the sweat and grime, he put the toga on. Then the messengers congratulated him, saluted him as dictator, and summoned him to Rome, explaining the terrible danger facing the army.

Fifteen days later, Cincinnatus had beaten the enemy, saved the army and returned to his farm.

1.15 What points about Cincinnatus does the story stress?

1.16 Compare the size of Cincinnatus' farm with your school sports' field.

1.17 Look at the picture on p. 45. Why was a toga unsuitable for ploughing?

1.18 Is it sensible to talk about 'typical' Romans, or Englishmen?

Relief showing a farmer ploughing with oxen.

Another example of Roman character can be seen just after the massacre at Cannae. Polybius describes what happened:

SOURCE 1H

About 8,000 Roman soldiers who had been left to guard the camp during the battle survived and were taken prisoner. Hannibal allowed them to send ten representatives to the senate at Rome to ask for a ransom in exchange for their release.

When they reached Rome, the men begged the senate to pay the ransom money for their release. They claimed that as camp guards they had not been cowards in battle and had done nothing unworthy of Rome. They had only surrendered because the army itself had been wiped out. But the senators realised that Hannibal wished to weaken the fighting spirit of Roman soldiers. So they showed no pity for their fellow-countrymen, and refused to ransom the prisoners. 'Roman soldiers', they declared, 'must either win, or die on the battlefield. There is no hope of safety if they are beaten.' ...

When this was reported to Hannibal, he was amazed at the proud spirit of his opponents.

1.19 Which aspects of Roman character does Polybius emphasise here?

1.20 Remember that Hannibal's Roman prisoners had families and friends at home, all waiting for the senate's decision. What does this tell us about the authority of the senate?

Greek cities in Italy

While the little community on the banks of the Tiber organised its defences and fought to protect its farmlands from the hill tribes, a different kind of city could be seen in south Italy and Sicily. Since the eighth century BC, Greek colonists had settled on the coast. There they built fine cities, with well-planned streets and elegant temples. As Rome's wars drew her citizens south, they were influenced by the language and ideas of the Greeks.

By the time Hannibal invaded Italy, most of the Greek cities of the south were loyal to Rome, though many rebelled and went over to the Carthaginian side after the battle of Cannae.

SOURCE 1I

A bronze portrait head of a Roman. It is not certain who he is.

1.21 What decision would you take in similar circumstances? Give your reasons. Now prepare a statement in groups which one of the senators will make to the people waiting for the decision outside the senate house.

1.22 What character can you see in the face of the Roman in Source 1I? Does it agree with what you have read so far?

Greek temples at Paestum in south Italy. The Greek colony was founded about 650 BC, when Rome was little more than a cluster of huts.

1.23 Find out as much as you can about the Greeks, their ideas, art, drama, buildings and demo-cracy. `AT 1.5`

Romans' belief in their gods and their future

'The Roman state was held together by its religious beliefs', wrote Polybius.

After the defeat at Cannae `6` the Romans made Fabius Maximus dictator again. The first thing he did was to make sure that the people were worshipping their gods properly. He gave orders for special religious ceremonies, sacred games, new temples, feasts for the gods and a particularly large sacrifice for Mars, the god of war. From the earliest times, Romans had believed that mysterious powers controlled human life and all nature. Some power watched over people, animals, crops, homes, boundaries and the weather, in fact over land and water everywhere. Gradually people came to think of these powers as gods and goddesses, who looked human. By offering regular sacrifices and worshipping them correctly, the Romans hoped to keep the gods friendly towards the city. So when disaster struck, it was a sign that the gods were angry. Special offerings were needed.

The carving in Source 1J shows the sacrifice of a bull, a sheep and a pig. The Latin word for this special offering is *suovetaurilia*, which combines all three animals – 'piglambull'. The priest, with his head covered, is sprinkling sacred herbs on the altar fire in preparation. Sacrifices had to be correct in every detail, otherwise the gods would be angry. When possible they selected fine animals like these. Like most ancient peoples, Romans were very

superstitious, especially in time of disaster. The entrails of the sacrificed animals were carefully examined and priests used them to foretell the future.

SOURCE 1J   *The sacrifice of a bull, a sheep and a pig.*

1.24 Put into your own words what you think Polybius meant in the quotation at the start of this section. `AT 3.3`

1.25 Find out what other religions say about spirits in nature and the world around us. `AT 1.3`

The site of Rome

Romans also believed that the gods meant them to be a powerful nation and that they had chosen the site of their city. Livy tells the story of the founding of Rome in the first book of his History:

SOURCE 1K

When Troy was captured, the Greeks took their revenge on the Trojans, except for Aeneas and Antenor. . . . Guided by fate, Aeneas came to Italy. There his son founded a new city, Alba Longa, where he became the first of thirteen generations of kings.

But then the rightful king was driven out by his brother Numitor, who killed the royal princes and seized the throne. But the fates had decreed that our great city was to be founded and that our mighty empire was to begin. . . . Numitor gave orders for the twin royal grandsons to be set adrift on the Tiber, so that they would drown. But by chance the river was in flood, and the story goes that as the flood went down, the floating basket was caught in the reeds on the Tiber's edge. Then a she-wolf, coming down from the hills for a drink, heard the babies crying and gave them her teats to suck for milk.

When he grew up, Romulus, one of the twins, decided to build a city on the spot where he had been left to drown.

Romulus and his brother Remus being fed by the she-wolf. This carving, on the side of an altar, also shows the shepherds who eventually found the boys, and Father Tiber, the river god, watching the scene (bottom right).

1.26 How many times does the story refer to fate? `AT 3.1`

1.27 What legends do you know about your own town or country? Write a story about the beginnings of the town or city nearest to you. Try to include some people/events which were probably true. `AT 1.5`

1.28 Are legends 'just stories'? If not, what can we learn from them? `AT 3.6`

The gods of the Roman state

The chief gods and goddesses of the Romans usually had temples in the larger cities and, of course, at Rome itself. They were:

Jupiter (the Greek Zeus) king of the gods and sky god
Juno (Hera) Jupiter's wife, queen of the gods
Apollo (Apollo) god of the sun, the arts and prophecy
Diana (Artemis) his sister, goddess of the moon and hunting

Minerva

Jupiter

Apollo

Venus

Neptune (Poseidon) sea god
Minerva (Athena) goddess of wisdom and crafts
Venus (Aphrodite) love goddess
Mercury (Hermes) messenger god
Ceres (Demeter) goddess of crops and harvest
Vulcan (Hephaestus) fire and blacksmith god
Mars (Ares) war god
Bacchus (Dionysus) god of wine.

The City on the Tiber

Another Roman writer, Marcus Tullius Cicero, described the site more clearly:

> **SOURCE 1L**
>
> *The gods inspired Romulus' choice! He placed his new city on the banks of a wide river flowing steadily to the sea all year. So Rome has all the advantages of a coastal town and none of its drawbacks. The city can import all it needs by river.... Romulus must have foreseen that his city would one day be the heart of a mighty empire. Rome has strong defences and a steep-sided citadel.*

1.29 Follow the course of the Tiber on the map on page 2. How does the river help to make Rome a natural centre of communication in Italy? *(AT 1.4)*

1.30 We know that in ancient times the Tiber often flooded. Naples had a much better harbour. So was Cicero exaggerating when he wrote that 'Rome was well-placed to be the 'heart of a mighty empire'? If so, why? *(AT 2.5)*

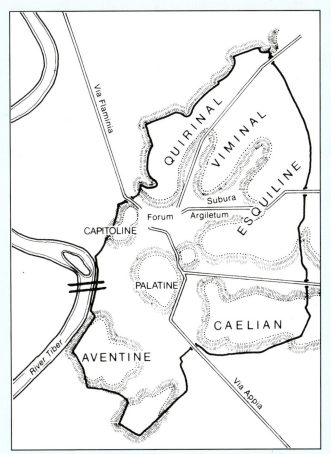

Early Rome, showing the seven hills and the surrounding wall.

Rome's first houses

Archaeologists excavating the site of ancient Rome found 'post holes' as they dug down. These holes showed where the original posts for the frame of the house fitted into the ground. We can tell what shape the huts were by looking at models made at the time as containers for funeral ashes (Figure a). So one of the first Roman houses probably looked like Figure b.

Figure a   **Figure b**

1.31 What problems would be caused by living in a house like this? *(AT 3.4)*

The Roman family

We have already seen how Romans respected their ancestors' way of life and the older living members of their families. The family was the basis of society. The Latin word *familia* had a wider meaning than our own 'family', and included the head of the household *paterfamilias*, his wife, their children, his sons' wives and children, their slaves and all their belongings! By tradition, the paterfamilias had complete power over all the members of his familia, and made all the important decisions about his children, such as their education, character-training and their marriages. By ancient law, the paterfamilias even had the power of life and death in his familia, and could, for example, insist that a sickly new-born child was left to die. But his wife, *domina*, the mistress of the house, also had a strong influence on the family. She ran the household, supervised the slaves, prepared the food and brought up the children. At home, the domina was respected and obeyed like the paterfamilias, but in Rome's early days she took little part in public life.

Like British women before 1918, she had no vote. But, as we shall see, it gradually became common for women to run shops and businesses and to share their husbands' crafts and trades. Some became priestesses, others received honours or inherited riches. And by influencing their menfolk, many women were able to play an important part in politics and government.

1.32 What are the modern equivalents of portrait statues? Is our attitude to ancestors different? If so, in what way?

AT 1.6

SOURCE 1M **A Roman holding the portrait heads of his ancestors. Wealthy Roman households usually kept portraits like these in the main room. They believed that their ancestors were still part of the family and often prayed to them.**

A Roman domina, or matrona, as she was sometimes called.

Roman government

It is not surprising that everyone respected and sometimes feared the paterfamilias. Romans also respected the city's ruling council, the *senate*. Senators were even called *patres*, the Latin word for fathers. Polybius thought that Rome was finally able to defeat Hannibal because the state was strong and her citizens respected it. In his Universal History, he explained how the Roman Republic had three strong elements which worked together:

SOURCE 1N

1 *Romans call their officers of state 'magistrates'. The consuls are the senior magistrates who carry out the senate's wishes and prepare the army for war.*

2 *The senate controls all public money . . . It sends ambassadors abroad and deals with foreign affairs . . . It can also declare war.*

3 *Finally, the ordinary people in their assembly decide all matters of life and death, give honours to those who deserve them and vote for their magistrates. They have the final word when a new law is made. . . . The strength of the Roman state is remarkable.*

Fasces

The most famous symbols of power for a Roman magistrate were the *fasces*. These were bundles of rods tied round an axe by leather thongs. They were carried by the magistrate's attendants, *lictors*, and showed his power to beat or even execute people.

Mussolini, the modern dictator in Italy (1922–43), chose the fasces as his emblem, and his political movement was called Fascism after them.

1.33 What does the term 'fascist' mean to you? Find out what you can about the movement.

AT 1.4

1.34 What symbols of office or rank can you recognise
a) in your own town or neighbourhood
b) in our national life?

AT 1.3
AT 1.3

Lictors, or magistrate's attendants.

Manpower and alliances

If we could ask Hannibal why he thought Rome was able to fight back after all the disasters, he would probably give two reasons.

First, Rome's manpower. If he had been fighting just the people of the city, his crushing victory at Cannae would have destroyed Rome's power. But Hannibal quickly discovered that counting Rome and her allies together, more than 700,000 men were able to fight as foot-soldiers, and 70,000 in the cavalry. And they were tough, determined fighters – even if their generals could not match Hannibal. Rome's enemies sometimes won battles, but Rome won wars. Her soldiers were well-armed, well-organised and adaptable, and they were fighting, as Polybius realised, 'for their children and country'. Less than 20 years after the disaster at Cannae, these same legions out-fought the most feared soldiers of their day, the Macedonians in Greece.

Second, Hannibal would point to the loyalty of Rome's allies. Though many cities in the south stopped supporting Rome after Cannae, most of the cities in central Italy stayed loyal throughout the war. This must have been hard for Hannibal to understand as he was offering them the chance to be free from Rome's control. We can see why this happened if we look at the agreements Rome made with her neighbours after the wars they had fought against each other over the centuries. Remember that in ancient times it was normal to destroy captured cities and make slaves of their people.

Here are extracts from some of the treaties of alliance, or agreements, which Rome made with the cities she had conquered:

SOURCE 10

Let there be a treaty of peace and friendship between Rome and the cities of Latium.

Let each have an equal share of the booty taken in wars they have fought together.

Let the people of Aequi become subjects of Rome, without being dispossessed of their cities or their lands.

The people of Aequi shall not be required to send anything to Rome except soldiers, when ordered.

Let the people of Lanuvium receive full Roman citizenship.

Let the Veliterni, who have enjoyed Roman citizenship for so many years, be severely punished because they have revolted so often. Let their walls be thrown down, and colonists settled on their leaders' lands.

11

1.35 Do you think that Rome was fair to the people she conquered? Give your reasons. `AT 1.6`

1.36 Make a list of the duties and privileges which Rome gave to the people of the allied cities. `AT 3.3`

1.37 Colonies were often placed near roads, river-crossings or mountain passes, or on the coast. Explain why. `AT 1.3`

1.38 The peoples of Italy had different backgrounds, traditions and languages. What effect did the colonies and roads have on Italy as a whole? `AT 1.3`

1.39 What effect does a new road have on the area it passes through? `AT 1.5`

There were several different kinds of allies. In some places all the people became Roman citizens. They were protected by Roman law, and had the right to trade, marry another citizen and vote. Other towns had fewer rights, but Rome promised to protect them and let them organise their own affairs without interfering.

Now study Source 1P, which shows the colonies and roads which the Romans had built by Hannibal's time, often with the help of their Latin allies.

Rome's colonies were often for ex-soldiers. They were sometimes 'new towns', sometimes built onto much older cities. Many of the colonists were Roman citizens, with full rights. The colonies themselves served many purposes:

- they guarded the land won by Rome and the allies

- they were prosperous trading centres

- they spread Rome's influence through the area.

Because of the new road network, armies and traders could move quickly and safely through central Italy.

Rome wins through

In the end, Rome was too strong for Hannibal. Even a genius could not match the determined Romans, their loyal allies, the numbers and skill of their soldiers and the intelligent leaders of the senate. Thirteen years after Cannae, Hannibal was forced to sail back to Africa, to defend Carthage against a Roman army. There, in 202 BC, he was finally defeated and the power of Carthage broken. He had been Rome's most feared enemy. Centuries later, mothers frightened their children by warning them 'Hannibal is at the gates!' His defeat was a turning point. After coming close to collapse, Rome on the Tiber was the strongest power in Italy. More important, Rome now had no rival in the western Mediterranean and was now a world power.

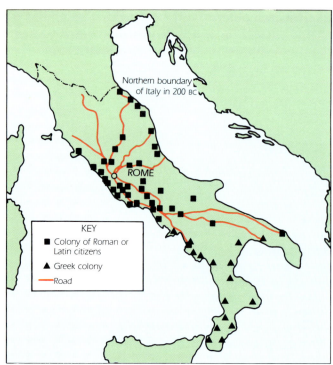

Bronze portrait of **Publius Scipio Africanus**, conqueror of Hannibal. Notice how the eyes appear to be staring. Discuss why.

SOURCE 1P **Roman colonies and roads in Hannibal's day.**

1.40 Look back through Chapter 1, then write a letter from one of Hannibal's senior officers, explaining to the Carthaginian government why, after his first great victories, Hannibal had not beaten Rome. `AT 1.5`

The new empire – government and benefits

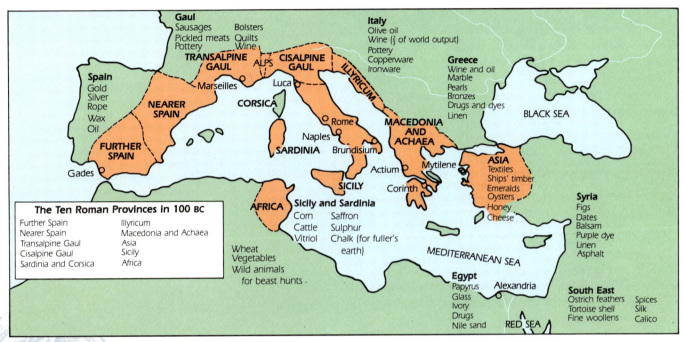

Map labels:

Gaul – Sausages, Pickled meats, Pottery, Bolsters, Quilts, Wine

TRANSALPINE GAUL · ALPS · CISALPINE GAUL · ILLYRICUM

Italy – Olive oil, Wine (⅔ of world output), Pottery, Copperware, Ironware

Spain – Gold, Silver, Rope, Wax, Oil

NEARER SPAIN · CORSICA

Marseilles · Luca

FURTHER SPAIN

Gades

SARDINIA · Naples · Rome · Brundisium

MACEDONIA AND ACHAEA

Greece – Wine and oil, Marble, Pearls, Bronzes, Drugs and dyes, Linen

BLACK SEA

Actium · Mytilene · Corinth

ASIA – Textiles, Ships' timber, Emeralds, Oysters, Honey, Cheese

SICILY

AFRICA · Sicily and Sardinia – Corn, Cattle, Vitriol, Saffron, Sulphur, Chalk (for fuller's earth)

Wheat, Vegetables, Wild animals for beast hunts

MEDITERRANEAN SEA

Syria – Figs, Dates, Balsam, Purple dye, Linen, Asphalt

Egypt – Papyrus, Glass, Ivory, Drugs, Nile sand · Alexandria

South East – Ostrich feathers, Tortoise shell, Fine woollens, Spices, Silk, Calico

RED SEA

The Ten Roman Provinces in 100 BC

Further Spain	Illyricum
Nearer Spain	Macedonia and Achaea
Transalpine Gaul	Asia
Cisalpine Gaul	Sicily
Sardinia and Corsica	Africa

After being defeated, Carthage surrendered her fleet to Rome and was fined a huge sum of money. Her empire was taken, and became the four Roman 'provinces' of Sicily, Sardinia plus Corsica, Nearer Spain and Further Spain. Rome was now the greatest power in the western Mediterranean.

So, when King Philip of Macedon threatened his Greek neighbours in 201 BC, the Greeks asked Rome to help them. The Romans defeated Philip's celebrated army. Next, King Antiochus of Syria invaded Greece. A Roman army chased him back to Syria. Then the Romans went home. They did not want any more provinces, where large armies would be needed.

This map of the Roman world in 100 BC shows Rome's ten provinces, and the products which they exported.

But there were never-ending squabbles around the Mediterranean. Rome was often asked to settle arguments. She used threats or warnings and sometimes harsher methods. In 146 BC Roman armies completely destroyed Carthage and the Greek city of Corinth. The territory of Carthage was made into the Roman province of Africa. Northern Greece became the province of Macedonia; Greece was scared into obedience. From now on the Romans set out deliberately to enlarge their empire. By 100 BC there were ten provinces.

INVESTIGATIONS

How Rome conquered Mediterranean lands
How the senate lost control
How one man seized power
How an empire was founded

Key sources
- Cicero's speeches
- Caesar's books
- Archaeology of Rome's Forum

200	180	160	140	120	100	80	60	40	20	BC–AD	20

BC 201 – Rome defeats Macedon
167 – 150,000 slaves reach Italy
146 – Corinth and Carthage destroyed
100 – Marius consul
82 – Sulla dictator
59 – Caesar consul
44 – Caesar murdered
27 – Augustus first emperor
AD 14 – Tiberius emperor

The senate and the government of the empire

The *senate* had been the town council of Rome. When Hannibal was defeated it became more respected. Now the senate governed an empire, and had more power, while the people had less and less influence.

There were 300 senators, all rich. When a senator died his successor was chosen by other senators. The *magistrates* were elected from the senate by the people's votes. They held office in Rome for one year. At the end of the year the senate sent them to govern the provinces. They stayed abroad for 2 or 3 years. Their duties were:

- to command the army stationed in the province to protect it

- to keep justice, often acting as judges in important cases

- to encourage trade, and see that the people were properly taxed.

The senate had no control over a governor in his province. He was only held back by his own conscience, and the fear of being punished when he returned to Rome for the wrongs he had done.

This painting from Ostia, the port at the mouth of the Tiber, shows a river boat being loaded with corn for the journey upstream to Rome.

The benefits of the new empire
Wealth poured into Rome as:

- **Booty and taxation** After a foreign country was defeated its riches were looted and shipped to Rome. The people of the provinces paid taxes to Rome, at about half the rate of modern income tax.

- **Slaves** When cities were captured in war the people were often sold as slaves. The Romans took more slaves than anyone before. When they conquered Epirus, in Greece, in 167 BC, 150,000 slaves were shipped to Italy. They became so cheap that even humble Romans could afford one or two.

- **Trade** Trade grew rapidly. Most of it was organised by Roman merchants. At least 5,000 Roman merchant ships were regularly sailing in Mediterranean waters.

Slaves

No one thought slavery was wrong. As well as war-captives, the supply was kept up by slave-traders and pirates.

Barbarian and uneducated slaves were used in farms or mining. They were often brutally treated. Runaway slaves were branded with a hot iron on the forehead. Well-educated Greek or Asian slaves were employed in town-houses as secretaries, teachers, doctors, ladies' maids or domestic servants. They were usually well-treated, and had a good chance of saving enough pocket-money to buy their freedom. Ex-slaves were called *freedmen* and *freedwomen*. They could set up their own businesses, and some held important official posts when the emperors ruled.

Roman law regarded slaves as things, not people. Judges only accepted a slave's evidence in court if he had given it under torture.

In a farming handbook one writer lists three types of farm equipment.

> SOURCE 2A
>
> *The kind that speaks (slaves), the kind that cannot speak (cattle) and the kind without a voice at all (ploughs, etc.).*

2.1 Why do you think slavery is wrong?

2.2 Find out about servants in Victorian times. How different were their lives from the lives of slaves in a good Roman household?   AT 1.3

2.3 Some people believe that the Romans did not invent or develop machines because they always had slaves to work for them. Discuss the good and bad points of owning slaves.   AT 1.1

Faults in the new empire

The upper classes made most of the new wealth. Only they were rich enough to buy ships and cargoes, and to profit from trade.

Most ordinary people made their living by farming. Look at these facts:

- Thousands of Italian peasants had to leave their farms to fight overseas or do garrison duty in the provinces. The average term of army duty was seven years. When at last they came home their farms were ruined. Few had enough energy or money to restore their land.

- Merchants imported cheap corn into Rome from Sicily and north Africa. Many Italian small-holders could not compete, and had to sell their farms.

- Rich landowners made large estates from these small farms. These were not worked by free countrymen, but by gangs of foreign slaves.

As a result a huge number of men, women and children flocked to the cities, especially Rome, to find casual work. Most of them were discontented, unemployed, and lived by begging.

2.4 What would be the feelings of the poor towards a) the rich, b) the slaves?

AT 1.2

Mithras slaying a bull. Soldiers drank the blood of bulls sacrificed in Mithras' temple, believing that they also took in some of the bull's strength.

Marius challenges the senate

Gaius Marius, a junior officer and senator, persuaded the people to make him *consul*, and to put him in command of a Roman army fighting in Africa. Though he won the war, Marius realised that an army of farmers who were anxious to return to their farms was not good enough. He set out to re-organise it.

New ideas and habits

Rich men got the habit of spending huge sums on jewellery, works of art, luxurious houses or ornamental furniture. They also met intelligent Greeks like Polybius ◁2 and read Greek literature. Educated Romans started to discuss new ideas, about personal freedom and behaviour, or government by democracy. New religions arrived, like the worship of the Greek wine god Dionysus, or Mithras, the soldiers' god from further east. Romans began to wonder whether their traditional customs and ideas, 'the ancestors' way of life' ◁5 , were as good as they had believed. One poet wrote 'Captive Greece has taken her conqueror prisoner'.

New laws made extravagance and revolutionary ideas illegal, but no one took much notice. Ambitious men began to be disloyal to the senate. They now aimed at winning power for themselves.

Gaius Marius (157–86 BC).

The new army

Marius encouraged men without property to join the army as a career. He gave them new uniforms and weapons, and insisted on strict fitness training. For months they had to practise using javelins and swords, and digging trenches, before they were allowed to join the legions. This professional army was ready to serve overseas for as long as necessary.

Loyalty of the army

Marius created an efficient army, but there was one problem. In the old days property-owning soldiers had farms to return to. Now soldiers had nothing when they were discharged. As a pension, they wanted small farms to live on, but the senate refused to set up any pension scheme. From now on soldiers had to rely on their commanders to persuade the senate to grant them land. As a result, they were loyal to these commanders, not to the senate or the people.

2.5 Can you imagine why the senate had not organised a pension scheme for old soldiers? `AT 1.2`

2.6 How are pensions paid today? Why could the Romans not pay pensions in the same way? `AT 1.3`

Marius' new army

The basis of the army was the *legion*:
each legion had ten *cohorts*
each cohort had six *centuries*
each century had 80–100 men.

Galea (helmet)
Pilum (javelin)
Lorica segmentata (metal strip breastplate)
Pugio (dagger)
Scutum (shield)
Gladius (sword)
Caligae (boots)

A model of a legionary from the Grosvenor Museum, Chester.

- The helmet was made of iron or leather.
- Curved strips of steel were laced onto a leather jerkin.
- The javelin had two parts, of iron and wood. The iron had a soft section near the head, so that it bent if it hit the ground, and was useless if the enemy tried to throw it back. Two were carried by each soldier: they were thrown at a range of about 20–30 metres.
- The sword was short and pointed, used for thrusting, not slashing.
- The dagger was used as a knife as well as a weapon. Swords and daggers were used in close fighting.
- The shield was made of layers of leather, with a metal rim.

The soldiers carried all these on the march, plus their personal belongings, and food for a fortnight. They carried digging tools and two lengths of stout timber as well which were used as posts in making a defensive wall round a camp. They wore stout hob-nailed boots.

2.7 How many men in   a) a cohort,
                             b) a legion? `AT 1.1`

2.8 Why do you think the soldiers of the new army were given the nickname 'Marius' mules'? `AT 1.2`

2.9 Imagine you are a new recruit: write a letter home telling your parents about your first month in the Roman army. `AT 1.5`

The power of the army

In 83 BC, the senate and people of Rome found out what a general with loyal soldiers could do. L. Cornelius Sulla was commander-in-chief of all Rome's armies in the eastern Mediterranean. He had just finished a long war against the powerful King Mithridates, who had invaded the provinces there and massacred thousands of Romans. But Sulla did not pension off his victorious soldiers. Instead he marched on Rome with his army. He slaughtered his rivals, and was made *dictator* – the first person to hold so much power since the war against Hannibal, 120 years earlier. Sulla was determined to make the senate once again into the united ruling council which had beaten Hannibal.

Problems of empire

Sulla strengthened the senate, and made laws to stop army commanders doing what he had done. But Rome still needed armies to control the empire, and soldiers were still loyal to their generals. So it was not surprising that ambitious men followed Sulla's example instead of obeying his laws. Meanwhile, in Italy and the empire, crisis followed crisis. Pirates raided coasts, stealing goods and selling the people as slaves. They seized merchant ships carrying grain to Rome and the people went hungry. Wars broke out in Spain, in Greece and, once again, with Mithridates in the east. New armies were hurriedly trained. New generals gained their soldiers' loyalty. But the worst crisis for Rome and Italy came in 73 BC.

COS = consul. Who is shown on this coin?

Spartacus

In 73 BC there was a break-out from a training school for gladiators in southern Italy. Led by Spartacus, the gladiators made their stand on Mount Vesuvius. Runaway slaves soon swelled their army to 70,000. Spartacus, who had once trained as a Roman soldier, used his fighting experience well. Rome's main armies were overseas. For

two years Spartacus' slave-army roamed Italy, killing and looting, easily beating the consuls and the hastily-collected forces the senate sent against them. In desperation the senate made M. Licinius Crassus commander. He had proved his ability under Sulla, and rapidly trained six legions. He smashed Spartacus' forces, and crucified 6,000 of the slaves along the main road from Rome to Capua.

2.10 What does this tell you about the senate and consuls?   AT 3.3

2.11 Imagine you are a young slave on a farm. If you run away there is nowhere to hide: you will be savagely whipped and branded if you are re-captured. What would make you join Spartacus?   AT 1.2

Gnaeus Pompeius Magnus (106–48 BC).

The remains of Spartacus' army fled north. They were crushed by Gnaeus Pompeius Magnus (Pompey), returning from a war in Spain. Crassus and Pompey now led their armies back to Rome, and demanded to be made consuls. The senate had no choice and gave in to the generals' demands, even though Pompey had had no experience as a magistrate. Again the army commanders had shown how powerful they were.

Gladiators

In this mosaic a Thracian has killed a retiarius (bottom left), while a murmillo (top left) is poised for the final blow. A heavily armed Samnite (top right) advances menacingly.

A sketch of gladiators fighting, drawn on a tomb at Pompeii.

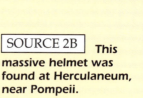

SOURCE 2B This massive helmet was found at Herculaneum, near Pompeii.

Some Italian tribes thought it was entertaining to make prisoners of war fight each other to the death. This brutal sport was taken up by the Romans. Criminals, slaves due for punishment, even volunteers, were sent to special schools, where they were trained to become professional killers. Gladiatorial contests were very popular, and ambitious politicians often paid for the fights, hoping that people in return would vote for them at election time. Julius Caesar staged a display with 320 fighting pairs in 65 BC, in honour of his dead father. One hundred and seventy years later in the emperor Trajan's time, one record gladiatorial show lasted 117 days. Almost 5,000 pairs fought to the death.

Gladiators were equipped in various ways: *Samnites* were covered from head to foot in heavy armour, with an oblong shield and a short sword: *Thracians* had a round shield and a sword or dagger: *murmillones* wore a helmet with a fish-shaped crest: *retiarii* wore armour on one shoulder, and used a net and trident. Men wearing the same armour were rarely matched against each other. Each fight was to the death, unless the crowd spared a brave loser. Successful gladiators became rich and famous, and could gain their freedom.

2.12 What modern sports contain physical violence and bloodshed?

2.13 What are your opinions about these sports?

2.14 Where can we nowadays watch scenes of violent death for entertainment?

2.15 What is the difference between these scenes and gladiatorial shows? AT 1.2

2.16 What type of gladiator wore the helmet in Source 2B? AT 1.1

Dangers of wealth

We have seen how rich men spent money on luxuries and used it to bribe people. Bribery at the elections in Rome was so common that it was hard to get elected without it. Hopeful candidates either gave cash to the people, or paid for extravagant shows to win popularity. They often used up all their money and went on to borrow huge sums. They repaid their debts when they became the governors of provinces by robbing the provincials. A governor, they said, had to make *three* fortunes out of his province, one to repay what he had spent on getting elected, another to bribe the jury when he got back to Rome and a third to live on afterwards!

Cicero, a young lawyer who later became a famous orator, summed up the result of this behaviour:

SOURCE 2C

All the provinces are in mourning: there isn't a place which has not been invaded by the greed and injustice of our fellow Romans . . . It is hard to find words to say how much foreign nations hate us, because of the outrageous behaviour of the men we have sent to govern them in recent years.

2.17 What does this quotation tell us about Cicero? AT 3.3

In 70 BC Cicero was asked to prosecute Verres, the ex-governor of Sicily. For three years Verres had systematically robbed and terrorised the Sicilians. He even kept a fleet of ships to carry to Rome the treasures he had looted from rich people and cities. Anyone who protested was flogged, imprisoned or executed. Rome had no public prosecutor: the Sicilians begged Cicero to do it for them.

Verres was sure he would be acquitted because the jury would be made up of senators, and most senators hoped to make their fortunes in the same way when they became governors. Verres also had a fortune ready to bribe the jury. But Cicero investigated Verres' crimes so carefully, and made them so public, that the jury did not dare let him off. Verres went into exile without waiting for the result of the trial.

2.18 What would have been the feeling of a) the senate, and b) the people, about Verres' crimes? *AT 1.2*

These provinces, which Pompey organised, were so rich that they more than doubled the revenue coming into Rome.

Soon the senate had more worries. Pirate fleets were attacking ships carrying corn to Rome, and its price rose. In 67 BC the people wanted Pompey to deal with the pirates. The senate was horrified that Pompey should have an army again, but could not stop it. Pompey was given a special command, with a huge force of over 120,000 men and 500 ships. In brilliant combined operations Pompey's fleets and armies swept the Mediterranean clear in only 40 days.

Pompey was immediately given another special command, against King Mithridates ◁17 who had attacked Roman provinces in the east again.

Pompey wiped out Mithridates. He added new provinces and re-arranged the old ones so successfully, that Rome's total income was more than doubled. He returned to a triumph 21▷ in Rome in 62 BC. He had become the most admired and famous Roman of his time. The senate may have feared what Pompey would do next, but he disbanded his armies and retired into private life.

2.19 Why do you think the senate was afraid of Pompey being in command of an army? *AT 1.6*

2.20 Why were these 'special commands' dangerous for Rome? *AT 1.3*

A tax-collector counts the coins, while the duffle-coated farmers wait to hand in their payments. This carving was found in Germany.

19

Julius Caesar

One of the few senators who had spoken in favour of Pompey was a rising politician called Julius Caesar. He was Marius' nephew, and a favourite of the people, but also may have had a private reason. He had once been captured by pirates and held to ransom. There is a story that he heard they were asking for a great sum of money: he laughed and said 'You don't know who I am. I'm worth much more than that!' The story may or may not be true: it *is* true that when the ransom was paid he collected ships, captured some of the pirate vessels and crucified the crews.

Caesar had been following a normal political career. Then in 63 BC the Pontifex Maximus, the High Priest of Rome, died. Caesar was thought much too young and quite unsuitable, but with the help of great bribery he was elected. He then became *praetor* and, in the next year, governor of Spain, where he defeated rebellious tribes.

2.21 Caesar was in Spain for a year. What does this tell you about his duties as High Priest of Rome?   AT 1.2

2.22 Do you think a priest of any sort in this country could lead an army in battle?   AT 1.3

Caesar's greatness

Caesar was elected consul for 59 BC with the help of Crassus and Pompey. Crassus was the richest man in Rome and his money bribed the people to vote for Caesar. Pompey called his veteran troops into Rome to vote.

As consul Caesar had a busy year. Some of his laws repaid Pompey and Crassus for their help, or safeguarded his own future. Others were genuine reforms, and one tried to provide fairer treatment for provincials. Even after the Verres case the senate had still done nothing to stop governors robbing the provinces. Caesar himself had made a fortune in Spain, but he knew that the robbery must be checked.

An Arranged Marriage

To strengthen their alliance, Caesar gave his daughter Julia to Pompey in marriage. She even had to break off her engagement to someone else. Though the marriage was no love match to start with, they

did become very fond of each other. Both Pompey and Caesar were broken hearted when Julia died in 54 BC.

2.23 Such arranged marriages were common among Roman aristocrats; are there any similar marriages today? Discuss Julia's possible feelings about the arrangement.   AT 1.5

The bride, who was often about 14, wore a special orange veil. The couple clasped hands to make their vows. The groom here is holding the marriage contract.

Caesar in Gaul

The people had given Caesar the huge provinces of Illyricum, Transalpine Gaul and Cisalpine Gaul and an army of four legions. He went there at the end of 59 BC.

In nine years Caesar conquered the rest of Gaul, though he had no real excuse for attacking it. He even made two short expeditions to Britain, in 55 and 54 BC. Caesar's book about this can still be read today. This is part of what he wrote about the Britons:

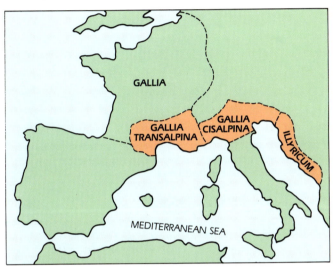

These were Caesar's provinces and the country of Gaul (Gallia) which he conquered.

SOURCE 2D

They use bronze or gold coins, or iron bars of a fixed weight instead. Tin is mined inland, and small amounts of iron near the coast: they import copper. There is every kind of tree, as in Gaul, except beech and fir. They think it wrong to eat hares, chickens or geese, but breed them as pets.

The most civilised people live in Kent . . . Most people further inland do not grow corn, but live on milk and meat, and wear clothes made of animal skins. All the Britons dye their skin blue with woad, which makes them look more terrifying in battle. They do not cut their hair, but shave all the body except their head and upper lip. Wives are shared between groups of ten or twelve men, usually brothers, or fathers and sons. A child is reckoned to belong to the man its mother married first.

2.24 Some of these facts are true, and Caesar saw them for himself. But others, which he heard from other people, are wrong. Which do you think are the true facts? AT 3.3

Celebrating a triumph

The day of a general's *triumph* was a public holiday. A procession passed through streets of cheering crowds. Marching soldiers carrying victory placards led the way, followed by wagons loaded with riches and weapons taken from the enemy. Military bands mingled with gangs of prisoners and chains, and white bulls ready for sacrifice. Captive chieftains in carts were gloomily aware that they would be strangled by night-fall. Near the end came the general in a golden chariot. His cheeks were painted crimson, and he wore a purple toga embroidered in gold. But a slave constantly whispered in his ear, 'Remember you are a mortal!' Senators brought up the rear. Finally the general sacrificed in Jupiter's temple.

2.25 Can you think of occasions today when processions anything like this are held? AT 1.3

2.26 This Roman procession was the original meaning of the word 'triumph': what does the word mean today? AT 1.3

Civil war

While Caesar was in Gaul, Crassus had died. Julia's death weakened the bond between Pompey and Caesar, and Pompey had become friendly with the senate. In 50 BC they ordered Caesar to disband his army. Caesar thought his enemies would kill him if he did. So he took the vital step of crossing the tiny river Rubicon, the southernmost boundary of his province, and invaded Italy. He made himself an outlaw by doing this. Pompey and many senators fled to Greece. There they collected an army as big as Caesar's. Another civil war had started.

Caesar crossed to Greece in 48 BC: his experienced troops quickly defeated Pompey, who was killed soon afterwards. He won other great battles against the senate's generals over the next five years. By 45 BC he had defeated all his enemies. He held four great triumphs in succession. He had no rivals.

The rule of Caesar

Caesar was still the people's hero. They had made him dictator five times since he had **crossed the Rubicon**. Though he was mostly abroad fighting, when in Rome he was a wise ruler as well as a great general. Caesar had seen more of the provinces than any other Roman. Remembering the problems of the provincials, and of the unemployed, he founded nearly twenty new cities in the provinces. In these *colonies*, as they were called, soldiers who had finished their service, together with poor Romans, were given land, seed and cattle to help them to start farming. He again improved the government of the provinces, and made taxes much fairer.

2.27 What effect do you think these new colonies had on a province? *(AT 1.4)*

Caesar provided work in Rome by ordering many new buildings, and new trunk roads in Italy. He insisted that one third of all the farm-workers on the great estates should be free men, instead of slaves. He started a public library system, to hold every book of Greek and Latin literature. Traffic jams became so frequent that he banned all carts during the daytime except builders' wagons.

The Roman calendar was inaccurate, so Caesar introduced a new calendar borrowed from the Egyptians, with 365 days in a year and a leap year every fourth year, which corrected the mistakes. We still use this *Julian Calendar*. Some slight adjustments were made by Pope Gregory XIII in AD 1582, and adopted in Britain in AD 1725.

2.28 In early times the Roman year began on March 1st. How have the Latin words septem (7), octo (8), novem (9) and decem (10) affected our calendar? *(AT 1.3)*

Honours for Caesar

Caesar's soldiers loved him because he won their battles, and shared their dangers. As he rewarded them with money, and farms when they retired, their loyalty was strong.

The senators were also anxious to show their respect. They loaded Caesar with many extraordinary honours, for example:

- his statue was placed in all Rome's temples

- he was named *Pater Patriae* (Father of the Country) and *Liberator*

- he was allowed to wear a purple toga and a laurel wreath (which he liked especially, because he hated being bald) and to use a gilded chair

- the month Quinctilis was renamed Julius (July).

Just before he died Caesar was made Dictator for Life: which word indicates this? You can also see the laurel wreath which hid his baldness.

Caesar as Dictator

People began to think things had gone too far. Caesar tried to refuse some honours, but the flattery affected him, and he was sometimes arrogant. Once he did not stand up when a group of senators came to see him. The senators objected that every proposal he made became law, and did this even when the proposals were sensible. Caesar made some Gallic noblemen into senators, so that the provinces could begin to share in government and this made the senate even angrier. The last straw came in February 44 BC when Caesar had himself made *Dictator for Life*.

Caesar saw that the senate and people of Rome were too selfish and irresponsible. Only a single man, backed up by a loyal army, could govern the huge empire. So Caesar chose to be a dictator. We know that Caesar had many more plans. Perhaps one would have brought in a new form of government.

But on 15 March, the day the Romans called the Ides of March, Caesar was brutally stabbed to death by a group of senators. Some had joined the plot because they were jealous, others like Marcus Brutus (Shakespeare calls him an honourable man) thought that Caesar's dictatorship had taken away their freedom for ever.

2.29 Do you think Caesar became dictator to improve the government of Rome, or for his own ambitions? *(AT 1.2)*

2.30 In what countries during this century has a dictator taken over the government? *(AT 1.3)*

This is Marcus Junius Brutus (c. 85–42 BC) who led the conspiracy to kill Caesar. The reverse of the same coin shows two daggers placed each side of the conical felt cap, which slaves wore when being freed.

After Caesar

The plotters hoped that they had given back its ancient position to the senate. But Caesar's successors remembered how he had used his army to seize and hold on to power. His heir, Octavian, and the consul Mark Antony took over Caesar's armies, and soon defeated Brutus and his colleagues. They divided up the empire. Octavian ruled Italy and western provinces, Antony the east. Here Antony fell in love with Cleopatra, queen of Egypt.

Octavian and Antony soon became rivals. After one more bitter civil war Antony and Cleopatra committed suicide. Octavian took over Egypt, with its fantastic wealth, as his personal property. He discharged 32 legions, over 150,000 men, and used his wealth to give them money and buy them land. The remaining 28 legions were needed to keep peace and protect the frontiers.

The first emperor, Augustus

What was Octavian to do now? His problem was this:

- if he remained in command of the army, as a dictator like Julius Caesar, he might be assassinated like Julius Caesar.

- if he gave up command of the army, and became a private citizen, another army-commander might use the troops to seize power, and so start another series of civil wars.

2.31 Would a democracy like ours have been possible in the Roman empire? AT 1.3

Octavian was not going to give up. He enlarged his bodyguard, the *Praetorian Guard*, to 9,000 men. As well as guarding Octavian they kept order, like a modern police force. He gave the rest of his soldiers better pay, and officers he could trust. They were spread out in forts along the frontiers in the provinces.

2.32 Why was it a good idea to keep the legions spread out? AT 3.3

Octavian and the senate

Octavian had to make sure that no group of senators should resent his position so strongly as to want to kill him. So, at a meeting of the senate he resigned all his powers and provinces. The republic was, to the Romans, all that was best in the old tradition. Octavian claimed that he had 'restored the republic'.

At once some senators, who had planned it beforehand, loudly begged him not to desert them. More joined in. Finally, when they all appealed to him, he 'reluctantly' gave way. He agreed to remain consul, and to administer the three provinces of Spain, Gaul and Syria for ten years. The senate was to govern all the rest. (Octavian's three provinces contained 22 of the 28 legions!) He kept Egypt. He was given the name 'Augustus' which means something like 'Your Majesty', with a religious feeling as well, and the month of Sextilis was renamed August(us).

Everyone was satisfied. Augustus could claim that his powers were not exceptional, because they had been *legally* given to him, for a limited period. Men conveniently forgot that no one before Augustus had held so much power at once. They could pretend that Augustus was not their ruler, but only 'first among equals'. The senate still met, and the people elected the magistrates, even though Augustus was allowed to approve some of them first!

Senators helped to govern the growing empire. About twenty of them formed a special 'cabinet' to help and advise Augustus. There were plenty of opportunities for ambitious men.

The empire in AD 14.

The emperor Augustus as a general, addressing his troops. He is wearing ceremonial armour.

Augustus and the people

With the treasures of Egypt Augustus also satisfied the ordinary people. He ordered many new buildings to be started, and many old ones to be replaced, so that there was plenty of work. He kept the poor people happy with gifts of money, and entertainments like chariot racing and gladiatorial shows. Yet he also tried to bring back the honourable ways of the old republic, passing laws forbidding extravagance and adultery, for example.

2.33 It was said of Augustus that 'he found Rome made of brick, and left it made of marble'. What does this mean?   AT 3.1

A larger safer empire

Augustus added new provinces to the empire. He wanted natural frontiers – the sea and the Rhine and Danube in the west and north, and the deserts in east and south. Behind the new frontiers, which the armies guarded, the provinces were governed sensibly, under fair laws. Thousands of miles of new roads were built, and new towns sprang up along them. Trade grew rapidly, for there were no frontiers or customs barriers to hinder it.

2.34 Why did Augustus want natural frontiers for the empire?   AT 1.3

2.35 Compare the empire at this time with the European community today.   AT 1.2

The next emperor

Augustus was always helped and encouraged by his wife Livia. She was as popular with the army and people as her husband. Augustus knew that the next emperor would be immediately accepted if he came from their family: outsiders struggling for power would only bring civil wars. But Augustus had no son. His nephews and grandsons all died before him, or proved unsuitable. So he shared his powers and responsibilities with Tiberius, Livia's son from an earlier marriage. When Augustus died Tiberius became the next emperor without trouble.

2.36 For what other reason might Augustus have wanted a member of his family to succeed him?   AT 1.3

Augustus ruled fairly and wisely for 45 years and died in AD 14. Anyone old enough to remember Rome before Augustus would only remember the civil wars, and the thousands who had died in them. Augustus had given them peace and prosperity. They were grateful, and no one dared to object when he was given extra powers as the years went by.

2.37 Had the Romans lost their freedom?

2.38 Do you think it is worth losing some of your freedom if you have peace and prosperity in exchange? Prepare speeches for a class debate on this subject.

Rome's emperors

How men became emperors

After Augustus the next four emperors were selected because they were members of Augustus' family. Gaius insulted an officer of the *Praetorian Guard* who killed him. The Guard, rioting through the palace, found Gaius' uncle Claudius hiding behind a curtain, and forced the senate to accept him as emperor. Nero, Claudius' stepson, was only sixteen when Claudius died and he succeeded him.

On Nero's death four generals marched on Rome. Each was made emperor when he got there, but was killed by the next to arrive. Last was Vespasian. His sons Titus, then Domitian, became emperors. Then again there was no son to follow. So the senate chose a sensible senator, called Nerva, as the next emperor. He invented a clever system: each emperor, known as the *Augustus*, chose a younger man as his junior colleague, called the *Caesar*. The Augustus trained the Caesar to take over when he died. The Caesar became the Augustus, and picked another Caesar, and so on.

Marcus Aurelius chose his son Commodus as Caesar. Commodus spent his time enjoying himself in Rome. He renamed the city Commodiana.

When Commodus was assassinated the Praetorian Guard chose Pertinax, but killed him because he was too strict. They *sold* the throne to the highest

The Praetorian Guard could make and unmake emperors.

bidder, who lasted only three months. Then three generals fought for the throne: Septimius Severus won. He spent the last three years of his life in Britain: his dying words to his sons were – 'Stick together, spend your money on the soldiers, don't bother about anyone else!'

Severus' son Caracalla killed his younger brother, to avoid sharing the throne. Caracalla was in turn murdered by the captain of the Praetorian Guard, who made himself emperor. Between AD 217 and 284 over 50 Augusti or Caesars had been nominated by one army or another. One died of plague, one was captured by the Persians. All the rest met violent deaths. By this time the senate was insignificant: real power was held by the army.

What emperors could do – 'absolute power'

No one has ever been so rich and powerful as the Roman emperors. Backed up by the army and Praetorian Guard they could do what they liked. Gaius humiliated the senate and threatened to make his horse consul. He even thought he was a god, and built a temple to himself.

Nero murdered his mother, his half-brother and his wife. In Greece he ordered the Olympic games and all the other festivals to be staged in the same year and was awarded over 1,800 first prizes, 'winning' every event, even when he did not take part. When a fire devastated Rome, he built a palace in the ruins. (It had a 37-metre-high statue of Nero, nicknamed the 'Colossus': the Colosseum later got its name from it.) He was accused of having started the fire, so put the blame on the Christians. Thousands were thrown to the animals, or crucified, smeared with tar and set on fire to light up his gardens.

But most emperors used their power for the good of their people. When twelve cities in Asia Minor were ruined by an earthquake, Tiberius excused all their taxes for five years. He sent out a team of senators to supervise the relief, and gave the worst damaged city an immediate grant of 25,000,000 denarii.

Even Nero, after the fire, paid for all the rubble to be cleared away quickly. He ordered corn ships, after unloading their cargo, to dump the rubble down river. He fixed planning regulations for the rebuilding of the city. Streets were to be at regular intervals, and at right angles. The height of buildings was limited and fire-proof stone had to be used. House-holders were ordered to keep fire-fighting equipment in open view, not hidden away.

No matter how power-crazy the emperors were, most of their subjects in the provinces were well governed, under just laws. They never saw the emperors, and never heard of their strange antics.

The Roman emperors, 31BC–AD305

31BC–14AD	Augustus	
AD14–37	Tiberius	
37–41	Gaius (Caligula)	
41–54	Claudius	
54–68	Nero	
69	Galba, Otho, Vitellius and	*The Year of the Four Emperors*
69–79	Vespasian	
79–81	Titus	
81–96	Domitian	
96–98	Nerva	
98–117	Trajan	
117–138	Hadrian	
138–161	Antoninus Pius	
161–180	Marcus Aurelius	
180–192	Commodus	
193	Pertinax, Didius Julianus	
193–211	Septimius Severus	
211–217	Caracalla	
217–284	over 50 emperors	
284–305	Diocletian	

Under Nerva, Trajan, Hadrian, Antoninus Pius and Marcus Aurelius, the 'five good emperors', the empire got bigger and richer, and the people healthier and happier than ever before. The people, ruled with just laws, which applied to everybody, no matter their race or religion, called it a 'Golden Age'.

After Caracalla there was confusion. Often several generals proclaimed themselves emperor at once. They were so busy fighting each other that barbarians were able to pour over the frontiers and settle inside the empire. Plague and famine wiped out millions of Roman citizens. The population fell so much that even barbarians were enrolled in the army to keep other barbarians out. To pay for them huge taxes were demanded. Thousands who could not pay the taxes ran off to the woods to join gangs of outlaws, who lived by robbing towns and farms. Silver became so scarce that the emperors issued copper coins with a thin coating of silver in place of solid silver. Since they could not trust the coins, everyone turned to bartering, exchanging goods for other goods.

Finally Diocletian beat his rivals and became sole emperor. To prevent future army commanders seizing power, he divided the provinces into smaller sections, so that governors had much smaller armies. He also split the empire into a western and eastern half, each with its own Augustus and Caesar.

2.39 Which emperor was ruling when Jesus Christ was born? *AT 1.1*

2.40 How many emperors were there during the 2nd century AD? *AT 1.1*

2.41 List the emperors of the 'Golden Age'. *AT 1.1*

2.42 What important changes did Diocletian make? *AT 1.3*

2.43 Do you think the pictures below match the characters of the emperors? *AT 3.3*

Nerva

Vespasian

Hadrian

POCKETS VOTE FOR VATA

PARIS, WE ARE YOUR FANCLUB

History of an Italian town

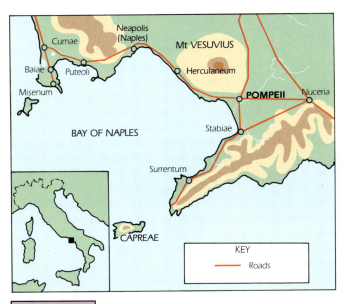

SOURCE 3A   The Bay of Naples area, with Italy inset.

KEY
—— Roads

SOURCE 3B   An aerial view of the ruins of Pompeii today, looking south.

ALL FRUIT SELLERS SUPPORT HOLCONIUS PRISCUS FOR ELECTION

Nobody knows for certain when people first began to live at Pompeii. But we can be sure that when Greeks were founding their colonies on the fertile Campanian coast they saw the advantages of the place, as you can see in Source 3A. It lay in the shadow of Vesuvius, near a river mouth, had a good defensive position, and was a natural trading centre for the towns and villages inland. Over the centuries, Greeks, and the neighbouring Italian tribes gained control of Pompeii. Finally, in about 300 BC, Rome captured the town, and Pompeii became an independent ally ◁12 . In 90 BC, however, along with most towns and cities in southern Italy, she rebelled against Roman rule. Sulla ◁17 crushed the rebellion and put a colony

of veteran soldiers there. Many townspeople were turned out to make room for the new settlers.

Gradually, Pompeii became a 'Roman' town, though many of its buildings, and its street-plan, were made to Greek designs. The civil wars brought bloodshed and confusion to the area, and Spartacus camped close to the town with his slave army ◁17 . But Pompeii prospered, and many wealthy Romans built villas nearby, attracted by the beauty of the coast. And when Augustus brought peace at last to the Roman world, there were even more new buildings and improved facilities to be seen.

INVESTIGATIONS

The streets and houses of Pompeii
What was daily life like?
What happened when Vesuvius erupted?
What can we learn from the disaster?

Key Sources
- The buried town: mosaics and wall paintings
- Inscriptions and graffiti. Shop signs
- An eye-witness account of the disaster

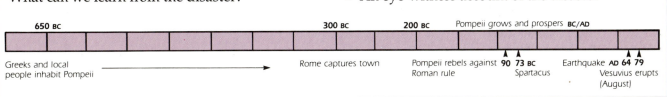

650 BC — Greeks and local people inhabit Pompeii — 300 BC Rome captures town — 200 BC — Pompeii grows and prospers BC/AD — Pompeii rebels against Roman rule 90 — 73 BC Spartacus — Earthquake AD 64 79 Vesuvius erupts (August)

IF YOU DROPPED DEAD TOMORROW? DO YOU THINK I'D CARE   · PLEASE DON'T WRITE ON THIS WALL ·

Look at the Sources 3B and 3C. Try to imagine the town and its people, in the first century AD. There were about 10,000 inhabitants. Some farmed fields outside the walls, some worked in the shops and taverns that lined the busy streets, others looked after their homes. The streets were narrow by modern standards, but straight with high pavements. They were laid out in a grid pattern. At crossroads there were 'stepping stones' for pedestrians, to help them cross the uneven and often dirty road-surface, and public fountains. These were supplied with water by a magnificent new aqueduct, which had channels into most of the towns in the area.

Most impressive of all were the town-centre, *forum*, with its fine public buildings, and the leisure areas: baths, theatres, amphitheatre and exercise grounds. Like many towns and cities in Rome's empire, Pompeii provided its inhabitants with excellent facilities and a good life-style.

In February AD 62, a terrible earthquake struck the region. One of the emperor's advisors wrote:

SOURCE 3D

Country houses were damaged beyond repair ... large buildings and temples in particular came crashing down ... the earth gaped open and poisonous fumes were emitted ... a flock of six hundred sheep was killed in an instant.

SOURCE 3C **An artist's impression of the forum, with Vesuvius in the background.**

Seventeen years later, on 24 August AD, after some warning grumbles, Vesuvius erupted.

Now look at the sources again.

3.1 Why were so many communities clustered round the Bay of Naples? *AT 1.3*

3.2 Why was Campania a particularly fertile area? *AT 1.3*

3.3 Look at Source 3B. Which buildings are likely to have been shops and which houses? (Compare with Source 3E.) *AT 3.3*

3.4 Source 3C shows how the forum looked in Augustus' time. In the forum, or nearby, stood many important public buildings: temples, municipal offices, the council chamber, a public speakers' platform, law-courts and markets. Make a list of the activities which took place in and around the forum. Use Source 3C as a reference. *AT 1.4*

3.5 The forum had many statues. Some were images of gods, others were portraits of men. What sort of men do you think these were? *AT 3.4*

A spring morning, AD 70

Titus Flavius Vespasianus was emperor at Rome. At Pompeii, Lucius Ceius Secundus, son of Lucius, was soon to go through a ceremony to become a man and his sister, Ceia, was soon to be betrothed. Lucius and Ceia lived in their family house a short distance from the main street of the town, with their parents and grandparents. Lucius was fifteen, Ceia fourteen years old.

It was an ordinary day. Lucius and Ceia got up as usual at the start of the first hour, just as it began to get light. It did not take them long to wash and dress: they were always glad to leave their rather cramped room at the back of the house. Breakfast was not really a meal at all: they snatched what they could find in the kitchen – a cup of milk or water, and a little bread, perhaps dipped in honey. Then they were ready for the day ahead.

Leaving Ceia looking out across their small garden from under the colonnade, Lucius crossed the *atrium* and quickly said a prayer to the household gods at the *lararium*. Then he helped the slave take down the bars from the front door. As they pulled the doors open, the hallway was filled with the din and glare of the street. Outside, the roadway was already full of wagons and the pavements crowded with passers-by.

As Lucius prepared to go to school, Ceia went to look for her mother. She was no longer a school-pupil. She could read and write well enough, and now she spent most of her day at home with her mother, learning how to organise the household. In particular, she was learning how to prepare food, and how to plan a menu for a formal evening meal. She had already found out that supervising slaves and looking after guests was not as easy as her mother made it look. Ceia knew that she would soon be betrothed and married; her mother's good advice would help her run her new home well. Though her schooldays were over, she still read the family's books whenever she could. She enjoyed poetry especially.

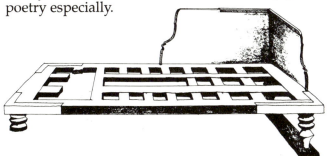

A bed, found at Herculaneum. Many Romans in fact slept on rugs or mats on the floor.

The lararium

The *lararium* stood in the main room of a house. It looked like a miniature temple, and held figures of the household gods, the *lares*. It was often decorated with pictures or designs. The head of the household ◁9 offered prayers and small gifts to the gods each day.

A lararium.

MAY THE MAN WHO STOLE MY GIRL BE EATEN BY A MOUNTAIN BEAR

THE MOTHER OF CAESAR AUGUSTUS WAS A HUMAN BEING

Comments, slogans and advertisements were written on walls all over Pompeii. Here are two examples: you will see several others later in this chapter.

3.6 Why did the Romans have a place of worship in their houses ◁7 ? Do we have anything like it in our homes today?

AT 3.2

3.7 What can we learn from graffiti like these?

AT 3.5

Houses

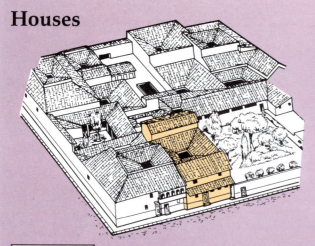

SOURCE 3E This drawing shows a block of houses as they would have been.

Pompeii's grid-patterned streets divided the town into blocks. Several houses and their gardens usually fitted into each block like a jig-saw. The illustration shows how Lucius' and Ceia's house fitted with its neighbours. There was no standard type of house, though many were similar. A shopkeeper usually lived with his family in a room behind or above his shop. Some poorer citizens had even less space. But Pompeii was a prosperous town, and so many families lived in comfortable and stylish houses. Some were very large. The house of L. Ceius Secundus, Lucius' father, was about average, and had most of the normal features. Here is a plan:

Points to note:

- Pompeian houses were normally single-storey. Lucius' house, however, had a few small upstairs rooms, recently added.

- There were few windows. Most of the light came from the roof-opening, *compluvium*, in the main room, *atrium*.

- Most of the rooms in Lucius' house opened onto the atrium. Beneath the compluvium a shallow pool, *impluvium*, caught the rainwater. The atrium floor often had mosaic decorations.

- The inside walls were painted in brilliant colours, with all kinds of pictures and designs. Even the garden wall in Lucius' house had a hunting scene painted on it. Some gardens were much larger, and contained statues, shrubs and fountains, surrounded by a colonnade.

- Romans had less furniture than we do.

3.8 What are the main differences between a Pompeian house and your own? If you had a choice, which would you prefer to live in, and why? Discuss this in groups. *AT 1.2*

3.9 Why are the houses designed to face 'inwards' with so few outlets to the street? Think about Italy's climate. *AT 1.3*

3.10 What use would the discovery of pollen grains from plants and shrubs as in Sources 3F and G be to archaeologists? *AT 3.5*

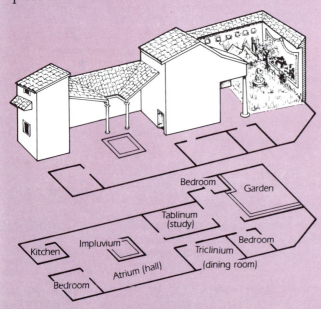

Bedroom
Garden
Tablinum (study)
Bedroom
Kitchen
Impluvium
Triclinium (dining room)
Atrium (hall)
Bedroom

SOURCE 3F This drawing and plan shows one typical house in detail.

SOURCE 3G A fine Pompeian garden. Archaeologists were able to identify pollen grains from the original plants and shrubs when they excavated.

Streets and school

To reach his schoolroom Lucius had to walk along the main street which ran from the forum to the amphitheatre. Here the tavern-owners and shop-keepers were taking down the shutters and arranging their goods. Ceia and her mother would also come this way later, on their way to the forum. The large central markets there gave them the biggest choice of food, and a chance to meet friends and find out the latest news. Everywhere there was the smell of bread and hot food for sale at bakers' shops and taverns: bakers had been busy well before dawn. There were unpleasant smells also, particularly where the fullers were treating their cloth: Lucius sometimes held his breath as he passed. The street rubbish stank too: the magistrates had been slack about the clearing up.

Ladders and scaffolding slowed Lucius down. They cluttered the pavement and sometimes blocked the side-roads completely. Builders were still repairing the earthquake damage from eight years ago. Much of the forum was still in ruins. Lucius remembered how frightened he had been at the noise and the way the ground moved.

When Lucius reached the schoolroom it was almost the second hour. As he settled down on the wooden bench to read and learn some more chapters of Livy's History, he was glad that he had only a few more lessons in this cramped and noisy place. His father had already made arrangements for advanced lessons with a new teacher, the *rhetor*; at last Lucius could concentrate on learning to speak well in public. In time, he could help with his father's business, present a case before the magistrate or even stand for election. But first he was going to receive the *toga of manhood*, the biggest celebration of his life so far.

As usual on a school day, the sixth hour was slow to arrive. But at last the teacher stopped droning and Lucius could go. Already the shops were closing and the mid-day siesta had begun. Everyone was looking for shade; for some, the day's work was over. As he walked home, Lucius was planning how to spend the rest of his day. First, *prandium* – lunch: some bread and a piece of meat from last night's dinner; then, meeting his friends at the baths.

The toga of manhood

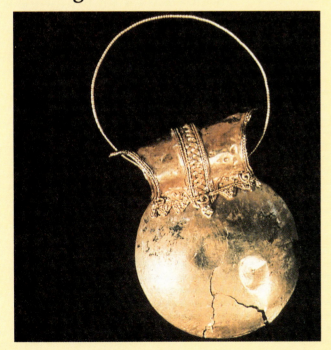

SOURCE 3H   **Bulla.**

Source 3H is a lucky charm, or *bulla*, given to a baby at the naming ceremony nine days after birth. When a boy was about fifteen, he presented this bulla to the household god, together with his childhood toga. This had a distinctive purple border. Then, in a special cermony, he put on the new, plain white toga of manhood, and went to add his name to the list of citizens. Relatives and friends came too, and joined the celebration: he was now a young man.

Men wore the toga on very formal occasions – council meetings and religious ceremonies, for example. But it was a heavy and awkward garment, and most people preferred the simple tunic. The toga looked dignified, however, and emperors encouraged people throughout the empire to wear one 66▷ .

3.11 Make a list of present-day 'coming-of-age' ceremonies involving young people in Britain and elsewhere. What are their special features?   AT 1.2

· PLEASE DON'T WRITE ON THIS WALL ·   · DO YOU THINK I'D CARE IF YOU DROPPED DEAD TOMORROW? ·

Schooldays

There was no law saying Roman children had to go to school, and children from very poor families rarely did. But most people thought it was useful to be able to read, write and do simple sums. So parents who could afford it sent their sons, and sometimes their daughters, to the local teacher. There were three kinds of teacher, and 'school' was usually a single class.

1 'Primary' school (7–11), where the teacher taught reading, writing and arithmetic. Pupils wrote on wax tablets with a sharp pen, *stilus*, and had to memorise and chant rules and tables. Girls often attended these classes.

2 'Secondary' school (11–15). Lucius' teacher concentrated on literature. Pupils, usually boys, studied the works of famous writers, read them aloud and learned them by heart.

3 The school of the *rhetor*, for older boys, taught public speaking. The pupil studied the great speeches of famous men, composed his own and practised all the time.

SOURCE 3I | **A teacher with a very small class.**

Many pupils left school after the first stage, and only a few went on to the rhetor's classes.

3.12 Compare the subjects taught and the teaching methods with your own school. What are the main differences? [AT 1.2]

3.13 Why did a girl's education stop so early? [AT 1.3]

3.14 Why was public speaking so important for an ambitious Roman boy? [AT 1.3]

3.15 Look at Source 3I. What is the boy on the right doing? [AT 3.3]

The Roman day

The Romans could measure time fairly accurately using water-clocks and sun-dials. But their normal method was to divide the daylight into twelve equal sections which they called *horae* – our word 'hour'. So a Roman hour had no fixed length, and was longer in summer than in winter.

SOURCE 3J

A Roman sundial.

3.16 Why do you think the Romans were satisfied with this rough method of measuring time? [AT 1.6]

3.17 The working day for most Romans started at or before dawn. How many hours work could they do by mid-day in the summer? [AT 1.2]

3.18 In summer, the mid-day break spanned the sixth and seventh hours. Why was it so long? [AT 1.3]

Earthquake

The carving in Source 3K comes from the *lararium* in a Pompeian house.

SOURCE 3K

3.19 The carving shows the forum at Pompeii. To the right is an altar and a bull being led to sacrifice. Look at the buildings and describe what is happening. Why is a sacrifice being made at this moment? [AT 3.3]

Afternoon and evening

At the eighth hour, Ceia and Lucius made their way to the baths near the forum: the complex nearest their home had not been fully repaired after the earthquake. There were separate entrances, and Ceia headed straight for the women's changing room; there she undressed and put on her bath soles. Then she walked to the 'warm-room', *tepidarium*, and sat down while she smoothed some specially scented oil onto her skin. Some of her friends joined her now, and they chatted as they got ready for the 'hot-room', *caldarium*. There the steam was so dense that it stung their throats and made it hard to see at first. Gradually they got used to it, and they all helped each other to rub on more oil, and to scrape it off gently. Some climbed into the hot bath and soaked for a while. At last, Ceia splashed herself with cool water from a bowl and went back to the changing-room. Near her clothes stood a small bath, full of cold water. Bracing herself, she stepped in, shivering as the water cooled her body. Now she could get dressed and hurry home to help prepare the evening meal.

In his part of the baths, Lucius had only just come indoors. He had been wrestling and playing ball-games with his friends, and had worked up a good sweat. They had taken a cool dip and were now heading for their *tepidarium*. The men's baths were larger and even more beautifully decorated than the women's section, but the routine was the same. Lucius and his friends passed quickly through the various stages, leaving the older men to relax in the comfortable surroundings.

It was the ninth hour when Lucius got home. His parents, grand-parents and Ceia were already reclining in the dining room, *triclinium*. No guests had been invited, so this evening meal was a simple family occasion. Lucius' mother was trying out a new local sauce with the main course.

It was getting dark, and the lamps were smoking: Lucius and Ceia were becoming drowsy. They asked permission to leave the triclinium. Tomorrow, they reminded their parents, was the festival; the theatre performance would last all day. And Paris, their favourite actor, was coming – they would certainly need a good night's sleep.

· DON'T PEE HERE · THE STINGING NETTLES ARE TALL ·

Baths

Most towns and cities in Roman times had at least one public bath complex, *thermae*. Source 3L shows the Stabian baths, near Lucius' house, before they were damaged by the earthquake. They covered a whole block, and had a large exercise area, *palaestra*, food and barbers' shops, bars and all the bathing facilities. Like modern leisure centres, baths were very popular meeting places: many people spent all afternoon there.

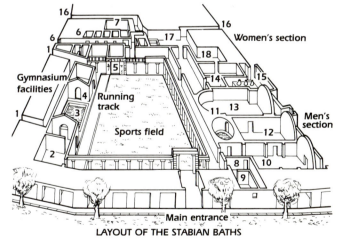

LAYOUT OF THE STABIAN BATHS

Exercise area
1 Private entrances
2 Pool washbasins
3 Swimming pool
4 Pool dressing room
5 Service area
6 Entrance and single baths
7 Latrines

Men's section
8 Entrance
9 Waiting room
10 Dressing room and cloakroom
11 Frigidarium (cold room)
12 Tepidarium (warm room)
13 Caldarium (hot room)
14 Laconicum (area with a high temperature, like a modern sauna)
15 Furnace and boiler area

Women's section
16 Entrances
17 Dressing room and tub for cold bath
18 Tepidarium

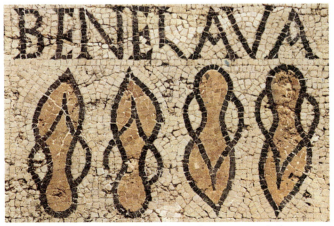

Bath 'soles' like modern flip-flops, from a mosaic in a North African *thermae*. The words mean 'Have a nice bath'.

 SOURCE 3L A plan of the Stabian Baths.

To heat the water and the hot rooms they used an underfloor heating system called a *hypocaust* which you can see in Source 3M. The floors of the warm and the hot rooms were supported on short pillars. A furnace heated the water tank; the smoke and hot air passed under the floors and up the walls of the hot room. Some private homes had hypocaust systems: in colder lands 64▷ , hypocaust heating was often installed in larger houses.

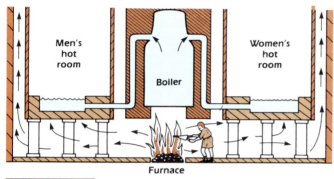

SOURCE 3M | A hypocaust.

· THIS PLACE IS GOING DOWN LIKE A HEIFER'S TAIL ·

3.20 What do you think of the Roman idea of having a bath in public? Give your reasons. *AT 1.6*

3.21 What do we learn about Roman engineering technology from the baths' water supply and the hypocaust system? What principles did they use? Why did most baths' main rooms have arched roofs? *AT 1.3*

3.22 In Roman towns, people could have baths in luxurious surroundings for a few 'pence'. Few private houses had bathrooms. Find out whether our Victorian ancestors were more fortunate. *AT 1.4*

3.23 Why do you think that bath soles were necessary? *AT 1.3*

Ceia's stola, a loose rectangular garment, caught at the shoulder. It could be tied at the waist.

Cena

Cena, the evening meal, was the main meal of the day, so there was more to eat, more variety, and it was a more formal occasion. Having friends for cena was a favourite Roman pastime. We read about some dinner parties where the host showed off his wealth by serving fancy dishes – roast flamingo, or stork pieces with blackbird breasts. But Romans ate simply too: most people could not afford anything else.

Romans used their right hands for eating. Slaves cut the food into small, easily-managed pieces, so knives were not needed. The cena had three parts:

- Starter course, *gustatio* – egg or seafood dishes with salads.

- Main course, *mensa prima*, which could have several different meat dishes.

- Dessert, *mensa secunda* – usually fruit and cheeses.

Romans spent a long time over their cena. Between the courses there was often some entertainment – dancers, for example, a recitation or a musical item. Wine was served too, throughout the meal.

3.24 Make a list of our formal eating rules. How different are our 'table manners' from the Romans'? *AT 1.2*

3.25 Potatoes, tomatoes and sugar were not known to Romans. What did they use instead? *AT 1.4*

3.26 We know much more about what rich Romans ate than about poor people's diets. Why do you think this is? *AT 2.6*

3.27 What can we learn about Roman food and eating habits from pictures and other objects discovered at Pompeii? *AT 3.4*

·TAKE YOUR FLIRTY EYES OFF SOMEONE ELSE'S WIFE ·

(This instruction was written on a dining room wall.)

Going to the theatre

Drama and theatre buildings were Greek inventions. From Hannibal's times, Roman writers had followed Greek examples in their tragedies and comedies. The earliest theatres in Italy were built in the south, where Greek influence was strongest. Pompeii itself had a permanent theatre 100 years before Rome.

The Romans took over the horse-shoe shape for their theatres from the Greeks too. But they built bigger stages and fixed backdrops, with pillars, statues and entrances. They also invented a stage-curtain which they pulled up from a groove at the front of the stage. Spectators at Pompeii had a canvas awning stretched above them to keep off the sun as theatre performances took place during the day. Attendants sprinkled the audience with scented water in the intervals!

But Pompeiian audiences in Ceia's time rarely saw the plays that the great dramatists of Greece or Rome had written centuries earlier. Instead, they preferred 'variety-shows', comic scenes, jugglers and acrobats, dancers and musical turns. Most popular of all was the *pantomimus*, like Paris. The word means 'someone who can act anything', and he was usually very skilful. The actor appeared in a mask and performed a well-known story, using actions but no words. A choir sang lyrics and musicians played. A talented pantomimus was the pop-star of his day.

SOURCE 3N

Pity the poor writer of plays, when his audience shouts 'Bring on the bears' or 'We want boxers' in the middle of a scene. (Horace)

3.28 Comment on the theatrical taste of the Roman audience. What were the alternative forms of entertainment? <18 49> Why were full-length plays less popular?

AT 1.6

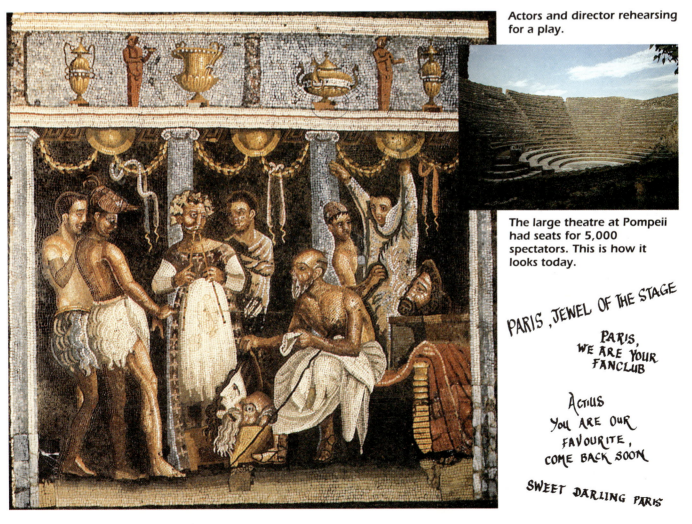

Actors and director rehearsing for a play.

The large theatre at Pompeii had seats for 5,000 spectators. This is how it looks today.

PARIS, JEWEL OF THE STAGE

PARIS, WE ARE YOUR FANCLUB

ACTIUS YOU ARE OUR FAVOURITE, COME BACK SOON

SWEET DARLING PARIS

Political life at Pompeii

Pompeians took their yearly elections seriously. All free adult males could vote for the town's two chief magistrates and for the other officials, who supervised the streets and public buildings. These slogans and appeals for support were painted, often very carefully, on walls all over town. More than 3,000 of them have been discovered.

3.29 What does the number of posters discovered tell us about the competition at election time?
AT 3.3

3.30 From these slogans, how do you think that political support was organised? What are the main differences between these posters and our own election advertising?
AT 1.2 /3.3

3.31 Why would a group of traders or craftsmen support a particular candidate?
AT 1.3

3.32 What sort of a person do you think Vatia is? Were these slogans really written by his supporters? Give your reasons.
AT 3.7

3.33 What part could women play at election time, even though they had no vote?
AT 3.3

· BARBERS SUPPORT TREBBIUS FOR MAGISTRATE ·

TEACHER SEMA WITH HIS BOYS RECOMMENDS JULIUS SIMPLEX FOR THE JOB

CURSE PEOPLE WHO SMUDGE PUBLIC NOTICES

ALL FRUIT SELLERS SUPPORT HOLCONIUS PRISCUS FOR ELECTION

PICKPOCKETS VOTE FOR VATIA
ALL LATE DRINKERS SUPPORT VATIA

CAPRASIA AND HER NEIGHBOURS ASK YOU TO VOTE FOR AULUS VETTIUS · HE DESERVES TO BE MAGISTRATE

EVERYONE WHO IS FAST ASLEEP WANTS VATIA ELECTED

SOURCE 3O

PROCULUS, MAKE SABINUS MAGISTRATE HE'LL DO THE SAME FOR YOU

A wall, with election posters.

How to become a councillor

N·POPIDIVS·N·F·CELSINVS AEDEM·ISIDIS·TERRAE·MOTV·CONLAPSAM A·FVNDAMENTO·P·S·RESTITVIT·HVNC·DECVRIONES·OB·LIBERALITATEM CVM·ESSET·ANNORVM·SEXS·ORDINI·SVO·GRATIS·ADLEGERVNT

This inscription was carved on the temple of Isis, close to the theatre.

Source 3P is an unusual inscription. Numerius Popidius certainly seems to have been a very young town councillor. Normally councillors were wealthy adults who had served for a year as magistrates.

Work out an explanation for this generous 'gift', remembering that:

1 Popidius' father had been a slave, but was now a very rich freedman.

2 Freedmen could not become town councillors but their sons could.

SOURCE 3P NUMERIUS POPIDIVS CELSINUS, SON OF NUMERIUS, AT HIS OWN EXPENSE, REBUILT FROM ITS FOUNDATIONS THE TEMPLE OF ISIS, WHICH HAD BEEN TOTALLY DESTROYED BY THE EARTHQUAKE. FOR HIS GENEROSITY THE TOWN COUNCIL ELECTED HIM A MEMBER THOUGH HE WAS ONLY SIX YEARS OLD.

3.34 How was Popidius' father hoping to secure a fine public career for his son?
AT 3.3

3.35 Councillors and magistrates were expected to spend their own money generously for the benefit of their town. Can you see any disadvantages with this tradition?
AT 2.6

Shopping

Many of the wider streets in Pompeii had shops along both sides. Often they were built into the front part of the larger houses, and rented out to ex-slaves of the household.

A shop usually had two rooms: a back room, which served as living quarters, and the front room, which was the shop and sometimes workshop too. It had a door and street counter or just a single opening, blocked up by shutters when closing-time came. Customers were often served on the pavement. Tavern keepers served their customers inside, though there was not much room to sit down.

There were all kinds of shops in Pompeii – butchers, bakers, potters, leather goods, ironmongers, coppersmiths, perfume sellers, sauce-makers, wine specialists, jewellers, furniture makers, cobblers, and many others.

3.36 How does an archaeologist work out
a) whether a building he uncovers was a shop,
b) what kind of a shop it was? — AT 3.3

3.37 There were many more bars and taverns than the town's population needed. How were all the tavern keepers able to earn a living? What does this tell us about the commercial life of this busy town and its ports? — AT 3.4

A Pompeiian lady

If you wanted to have your clothes cleaned or dyed, you went to the fuller. There were fullers' shops, with their vats, presses and stinking pots of sulphur, urine and soda all over Pompeii. The headquarters of the guild of fullers was a large and beautiful building opening onto the forum. This inscription was carved above its entrance:

> **SOURCE 3Q**
>
> *Eumachia, Public Priestess, in her own name and with her own money, built this porch and colonnade and dedicated them to the peace of the empire and the emperor's family*

3.38 What does this inscription tell us about Eumachia and her importance in the town? — AT 3.3

3.39 The fullers called Eumachia their patroness. Find out what this means. — AT 1.3

3.40 Inside the headquarters stood a fine statue of Livia, wife of Augustus and mother of Tiberius ◁24▷ Why do you think Eumachia chose to honour Livia in this way? — AT 3.3 /1.6

Shops in Pompei.

· A COPPER POT IS MISSING FROM THIS SHOP · 65 SESTERCES REWARD IF ANYONE BRINGS IT BACK · 20 SESTERCES IF HE TELLS US WHO THE THIEF IS ·

This notice was on the front of a shop.

Now look carefully at the illustrations:

3.41 How many different kinds of shops can you count, using the pictures? — AT 3.3

3.42 Find evidence for the way shopkeepers looked after their customers. — AT 3.3

3.43 Find the wine and oil seller. Where did the oil come from, and what was it used for in Roman times? — AT 3.3

3.44 What kinds of meat can you see in the picture on page 37? — AT 3.3

3.45 Look at the clothes which shoppers and shopkeepers are wearing. How many different kinds of garment can you see? — AT 3.3

3.46 Find the wine-bar. How did the owner try to make it attractive to customers? — AT 3.3

3.47 Using these pictures as evidence, work out which members of Roman families did the shopping and who served in or ran the shops. — AT 3.3

3.48 These carvings come from tombs, altars, temples, and sometimes from the shops themselves. What can we learn in general from scenes like these? — AT 3.3 /5

A view over the bay, 24 August AD 79

About 25 miles from Pompeii, across the Bay of Naples, lay Misenum, base of the Roman fleet. The admiral of the fleet was Caius Plinius Secundus (Pliny the Elder), who had a fine villa there, overlooking the bay. He was a scholar, a writer, and famous for his Encyclopaedia on Natural History ◁3. Staying with him at Misenum were his sister and her son Publius Caecilius Secundus, who was about seventeen. They were spending the summer, as many Romans did, by the bay, with time to read, walk and enjoy the climate and the peace. Years later, Publius wrote to a historian Tacitus 58▷ to tell him what happened that day.

An umbrella pine (and family tombs) beside the Appian Way. Pliny's nephew Publius would have passed this way while travelling from Rome to Misenum.

SOURCE 3R

Early in the afternoon, my mother showed my uncle a cloud of unusual size and shape . . . it looked like an umbrella pine: it climbed to a great height on a sort of trunk, and then spread out into branches. I suppose that this was because it was pushed upwards at the first blast, but as this pressure reduced and its own weight took over, it thinned out and began to spread sideways. In some places the cloud was white, in others stained and dirty . . .

My uncle knew at once that he must take a closer look. He gave orders for a boat to be got ready, and asked me if I wanted to come. I told him that I preferred to stay and study; in fact he had given me some writing to do. Just as he was leaving, my uncle received a message begging him to rescue those who lived near Herculaneum. So he changed plan: the scientific investigation became a rescue mission. He launched the warships to bring help to the many people who lived on that lovely stretch of coast.

He sailed quickly into the danger zone which everyone else was leaving. My uncle showed no fear; instead he observed each new phase of the eruption and got a slave to note down the exact details. Ashes were falling, hotter and thicker the closer they sailed, followed by bits of pumice and stones blackened by flames. Suddenly they were in shallow water, and the shore was blocked by debris from the volcano. The helmsman advised him to return to Misenum, but my uncle ordered the ships to turn south towards Stabiae, to rescue his friend

Pomponianus . . . He landed there, embraced his terrified friend, and to calm everyone else's fear by showing none himself, he had a bath and went to dinner . . .

Meanwhile on Vesuvius wide sheets of flame and leaping fires burst out in every direction . . .

My uncle went to his room and slept. People could hear him snoring. The courtyard outside his bedroom began to fill with ashes and pumice, and the level was rising so high that if he had stayed there any longer he would never have got out. So he was woken and came out to join the others. They discussed what to do: should they stay indoors, though the buildings were shaking and swaying, or risk going outside, where there was danger from falling pumice? They compared the risks and chose to go out, but they tied pillows on their heads to protect them from falling objects.

Everywhere else it was daylight by now, but near Vesuvius it was still dark – ever darker than an ordinary night. My uncle went down to the shore to see if it was possible to escape by boat, but the sea was still wild and dangerous. Someone spread a sheet on the ground for him to rest on, and he kept asking for cold water. The flames and the stink of sulphur made him stand up . . . he got to his feet, propped up by two slaves, then collapsed. I suppose that the fumes blocked his windpipe . . . When daylight returned on 26 August, 36 hours after the last day he had seen, his body was found, completely uninjured and fully clothed. He seemed asleep rather than dead.

A wall painting from Pompeii showing warships at sea. Vessels like these, but equipped with masts and sails, carried Pliny into the danger-zone.

'The fish feel their world shrinking, as builders sink their concrete foundations down to the sea-bed' (wrote one poet). The Bay of Naples was lined with luxurious villas like this.

Pliny's route with the warships, and the fall out pattern of pumice and ash from Vesuvius.

3.49 Pliny was a scholar and natural scientist. Which of his actions show his scholarly attitude? And which parts of the letter suggest that his nephew had similar interests? *AT 3.3*

3.50 What kind of person was the Elder Pliny, according to this account? *AT 3.3*

3.51 As historians and archaeologists try to reconstruct the last hours of Pompeii and Herculaneum, what help does this letter give? *AT 3.7*

3.52 Many people still live in the shadow of Vesuvius. Discuss why. Would you choose to live near an active volcano? List your reasons. *AT 1.3*

Younger Pliny's story

After the Elder Pliny's death, Publius inherited his uncle's estate. He also took his uncle's names, which he combined with his own, as Romans usually did. So he became Gaius Plinius Caecilius Secundus: we call him the Younger Pliny to avoid confusion. Tacitus asked him to describe his own experience of the eruption. This is what he wrote:

SOURCE 3S

Dawn came at last (on the morning after my uncle had left), but with a very faint light . . . The surrounding buildings were already wobbling, and if our house had collapsed we would have been in great danger. So my mother and I decided to leave Misenum . . . but even then extraordinary happenings terrified us. Our carriages began to slide around in all directions, though the ground was quite level. They would not stay still even though they were wedged with stones . . . We also saw the sea sucked back, apparently by the earthquake, leaving sea-creatures stranded on the dry sand. Looking towards Vesuvius, all we could see was a frightening black cloud, split apart by bursts of flame.

As we fled . . . it grew dark – we could hear women shrieking, children crying and men shouting. Some were calling for their parents, others for wives and children. Some prayed to the gods for help, still more believed there were no gods left, and that the whole world would be plunged into everlasting darkness. I thought the whole world was dying, and I with it.

3.53 You are an observant naturalist, like the Elder Pliny. Using the two letters, note down the main events and phases of the eruption.

AT 1.4

The eruption blew the centre from the volcano, leaving a crater 3.5 km across. Herculaneum was submerged under 13 m of lava and mud, Pompeii buried beneath 3–4 m of ash and pumice. At Pompeii, thousands died, but many escaped. Because the eruption started in the morning, many people were outside, and at work in the fields. Some who went south at once had a good chance. But those in town, especially the old, faced death in many forms, from fire and falling buildings. But the main killer was the fumes. Thousands were choked by the poisonous sulphur, then covered by a blanket of ash. Some suffocated as they huddled in their houses, others collapsed in the street as they fled. All died miserably. It was the greatest natural disaster in the history of Europe.

3.54 Imagine that you are Lucius or Ceia and have survived the eruption. Write a letter like Pliny's to a friend describing the disaster and what happened in the first few days afterwards.

AT 3.4

A mosaic floor, showing a fight between an octopus and a lobster, and many other sea-fish. Almost all of them can still be found in the Bay of Naples, including eels, prawns, bass, red mullet, dog-fish and squid. Perhaps this is what the sea-bed looked like during the eruption.

Postscript

In the days that followed, survivors went back to the ruins. They tunnelled through the ash and pumice, looking for precious objects and money. Looters found the forum and took away several bronze statues. Some searched for loved ones under the ash. But gradually the survivors drifted away. There was no rebuilding, and as time passed, people forgot about Pompeii. When Rome's empire disintegrated, a legend grew up about a buried city, but nobody knew if it was true.

Centuries passed. In AD 1594, workmen digging a water channel cut through to a ruined building, and found an inscription with the name POMPEIS on it. But they thought that it was probably a villa belonging to the great Pompey ◁17 and did not investigate. More time passed, until in AD 1748 the buried city was re-discovered. For almost a hundred years, different kings of Naples sent teams of diggers to see what they could find. These treasure-hunters unearthed many magnificent objects and destroyed much important evidence as they dug carelessly down.

But in AD 1861 Giuseppe Fiorelli was put in charge of the site. He carted away the rubble left by the treasure-hunters, cleared the streets and revealed the plan of the town. Then he numbered the blocks and the buildings so that records could be kept. Whenever an object was found, its position on the site and its depth in the ground were carefully noted down. Fiorelli's greatest discovery was the method of recreating the 'bodies' of those who died. The falling ash had gradually hardened round them. Over the centuries the bodies decomposed, but Fiorelli, by pumping liquid plaster into the cavity, recreated the original shape.

The eruption of Vesuvius in AD 79 was a horrifying tragedy for everyone who lived nearby. But the catastrophe, the ash and the lava have preserved for us a picture of everyday life in two Italian towns – trapped in time. We can see in Pompeii and Herculaneum what we cannot see anywhere else in Rome's empire, and certainly not in Rome itself – what life was like in the middle of a working summer morning, during the first century AD.

3.55 Explain in your own words the differences between 'treasure-hunting' and scientific archaeology.   AT 3.6

3.56 Why was Fiorelli's detailed record-keeping so important?   AT 3.5

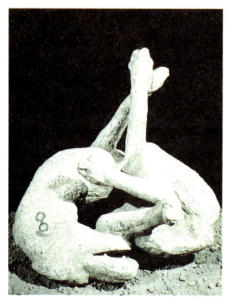

Plaster casts of the dead from Pompeii and Herculaneum.

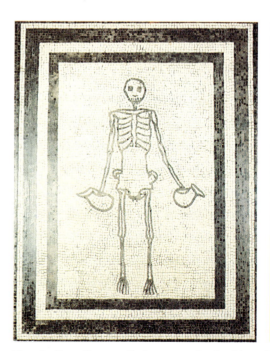

· INN KEEPER – DROWN IN YOUR OWN SEWER WINE ·

Mosaic floor from a dining-room in the Vesuvius area. The skeleton with the wine jugs reminds guests to enjoy life while they can; death is never far away.

Archaeology

We can still sometimes see remains of Roman bridges, town walls, houses or military camps. But many objects and buildings are buried underground in layers and have to be carefully uncovered by archaeologists. When a building was burned down, the rubble was not carted away. It was flattened and the new building put on top. In towns which have always been lived in, this happened often. Parts of Roman London are six or seven metres below the modern surface.

Things in the same layer will be roughly the same age. If a coin has the Roman emperor Claudius's head on it, we know that the layer cannot have been made before Claudius became emperor. Coins are not in use for very long. Look at any coins in your pocket and see whose head is on it. It is unlikely that any are more than twenty years old. Coins help us to give a date to a layer.

If there is more than one layer, the bottom one must have been put there first, so long as the layers have not been disturbed. It is like a dustbin; the things you threw away yesterday will be lower down than the rubbish you put in today, or tomorrow.

Archaeologists have to dig very carefully and slowly, so that they do not disturb the layers, otherwise some object may be recorded in the wrong layer.

From things like cooking pots or surgical instruments, jewellery or children's toys, we can guess how the Romans lived and played. But thousands of *inscriptions* have also been found: these are usually slabs of stone into which announcements, written in Latin, have been cut. They give us facts, such as who paid for a building to be put up, or they set out new laws. And from the thousands of tombstones of ordinary people we can tell:

- the average age at which men and women died
- how many babies women had, and how old they were when they had them
- how many children died as infants.

3.57 Look at some inscriptions on public buildings, statues or tombstones where you live, and see what information they will give to people living a thousand years from now.

Tombstone of Lucius Vibius, his wife and son. Note the family ears. What has happened to Lucius' teeth?

IV CAPITAL OF THE WORLD

Capital of the world

Visitors to Rome today are sometimes surprised (and disappointed) by what they find. Source 4A will help you understand why. Not much of ancient Rome is still standing. Over the centuries, earthquakes, fires and looters destroyed most of it. New buildings were put up: some contractors demolished old ones and re-used their stone and marble. Sometimes marble was thrown into kilns, and ground into powder to make lime for cement. Many statues and decorations were taken to different sites (and to other cities) to be used on buildings there.

So visitors need a guide book, and a good imagination, to work out what the centre of Rome was like when the emperors ruled. Source 4B gives you an idea how the city looked in about AD 250.

Trajan's forum

Augustus' forum

Colosseum

Capitoline Hill

Senate House

Forum Romanum

Arch of Titus

Palatine Hill

Emperors' palaces

Circus

INVESTIGATIONS

The city of Rome
Roman building techniques
Life in Rome and in the empire
How Christians were treated

Key Sources
- Archaeological remains and finds
- Statues, tombstones, coins and carvings
- Writers' descriptions: an emperor's letters

AD 100   Trajan conquers Dacia   AD 200

AD 14
Death of Augustus
'Marble Rome'

45
Claudius' harbour
and aqueduct

64
Great
Fire
of Rome

70
Titus
sacks
Jerusalem

80
Colosseum and Titus' arch

Builds forum/market
Pliny in Bithynia

Hadrian Emperor
Lollius (city prefect)

Septimius
Severus
Emperor

4.1 Study these pictures. Identify the ancient buildings in Source 4A.

Fortunately there are many ways to find out what Rome looked like in ancient times:

1 Through the work of archaeologists. For about 200 years, archaeologists have been digging and clearing the city centre. They find what is left of ancient buildings, and make careful records. They are still at work today.

2 Writers in Roman times often described the city's buildings. Source 4C gives one Greek author's description:

> SOURCE 4C
>
> After the temple of Jupiter had been destroyed by fire, Emperor Domitian built a new one. . . . the roof was covered in gold plate. Its pillars were made of Greek marble. When we saw them newly cut from the quarry near Athens, their proportions seemed beautiful.

4.2 What building does this coin show? Compare it with the original.

The historic centre

The buildings (and open spaces) in the centre of Rome amazed visitors from all over the world. Julius Caesar and the first emperor, Augustus, had restored the old Forum Romanum and each built a new one close by. As Rome's population and the empire grew, more and more public buildings were needed for government business and court-rooms. When Nero was emperor, a terrible fire destroyed many regions of Rome. So much re-building took place then that Nero called it his 'New City'. After Nero, first Vespasian, then Nerva and finally Trajan each built a forum on the north side of the Forum Romanum. Soon the whole area became a vast marble-covered precinct, with colonnades, temples, statues, civic buildings and a magnificent permanent market. But the old Forum Romanum still remained the heart of the city.

Rome's centre was not just fine buildings, however. Everywhere statues, carvings and inscriptions reminded passers-by of the great men of the past and their achievements – Rome's history carved in stone. A visitor approaching the Forum Romanum from the east along the Sacred Way passed beneath the triumphal arch of Titus. Further down the Sacred Way stood the temple of Julius Caesar, built on the spot where the dictator's body had been cremated in 44 BC ◁22, after the assassination. Facing the temple was the speakers' platform, decorated with the prows of ships, *rostra*, captured from the Carthaginians a in sea-battle. Close by stood the Senate House or *Curia*, where senators met to discuss government business and to advise the emperor. Senators looked very dignified in their purple-trimmed togas, as they walked through the forum. (Purple dye was extracted from shell-fish.) The emperor too might be seen, making his way down from his palace on the Palatine Hill.

> SOURCE 4D
>
> **The Ara Pacis – Part of Augustus' Altar to Peace, with the emperor's family in procession.**

Titus' Triumph in Judaea

Judea was a difficult province to govern. The Jews hated Roman rule, even though the Romans did not stop them from worshipping their god, Jehovah. Finally, in AD 66, all Judaea rebelled against Rome, and a bloody war started. After many years of fighting, Titus, son of the emperor Vespasian, captured Jerusalem (AD 70). He took the treasures from the temple, and when he retured to Rome, his victorious soldiers carried them proudly in his triumphal procession.

In Judaea, one group of Jews fought on. They seized a high rock fortress, Masada, and refused to give in. But the Roman army destroyed their defences with fire and battering rams. At last, the Jewish commander, Eleazar, realised that all was lost, and spoke to his followers:

SOURCE 4E

'We have sworn that we will not serve the Romans – only God, who is the true ruler of men. We cannot allow our women and children to become slaves – we must all die by our own hands, to preserve our freedom.'

Then each man embraced and killed his family. Next they drew lots and appointed ten executioners to kill the rest of the men. Then one man was chosen to kill the remaining nine. When he had done this, he stabbed himself and fell beside his family. 960 men, women and children died.

When the Romans soldiers entered the fortress they found the bodies. But they had no feeling of triumph: instead they admired the determination of the defenders, and their contempt for death.

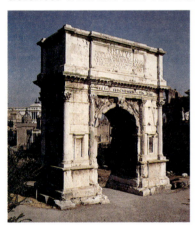

Titus' triumphal arch, as it looks today.

4.3 These events were described by a Jewish historian, Josephus. What do they tell us about the feelings of some of Rome's subjects, and about the problems of governing an empire? *(AT 3.5)*

4.4 What do you feel about events like these? Give reasons for your views. *(AT 3.5)*

4.5 Look back at Source 4D. What ideas and feelings has the sculptor tried to show in this carving? *(AT 3.3)*

Emperor Trajan's Rome

Trajan's forum and market formed a separate city-centre. It included two libraries, a temple, a basilica and a vast semi-circular shopping centre with a market hall and shops on many levels. Close to the libraries stood one of the most remarkable monuments in Rome, Trajan's column. The emperor erected this to celebrate his victory over the Dacians, who lived beyond the river Danube. Trajan ordered his stonemasons to carve scenes from the campaign on a continuous frieze which curls round the column in a spiral.

There is no full written history of Trajan's campaigns against the Dacians. To find out what happened, historians try to follow the story on the frieze itself. Some of the figures are damaged, but the carvings clearly show the legions in action. There are scenes with soldiers marching, building camps and bridges, fighting battles and besieging enemy strongholds.

Trajan's market. The Great Hall, with shops at ground floor and first floor level, as in many modern shopping arcades.

4.6 The illustration shows the bottom four bands of the column. Working upwards, try to find: `AT 3.3`
  1 the Danube river god
  2 a bridge built on boats
  3 what marching soldiers carried
  4 the different styles of shields
  5 men building a camp
  6 cavalrymen
  7 the emperor himself, addressing some Dacians from a raised platform

4.7 How do the Dacians differ in appearance from the Romans? `AT 3.3`

4.8 Why is this carved frieze so valuable as historical evidence? `AT 3.5`

4.9 What impression of the campaign do these pictures create? `AT 3.3`

SOURCE 4F Trajan's column reliefs.

Building and technology

The best architects, engineers and builders came to Rome to help with the emperors' building projects. They used the arch, cement and concrete and various tools and machines.

The Arch

Romans did not invent the arch, but they used it more cleverly than ever before.

4.10 Look at the pictures on pages 33, 44, 49 and 50. Listing the various buildings involved, find all the examples you can of `AT 1.4`

  1 a single arch as in Figure a

  2 two-storey arches as in Figure b

  3 a series of arches, side by side, making a vault as in Figure c.

Cement and concrete

Romans discovered that powdered limestone mixed with fine sand and water made a cement/mortar which held stones or bricks firmly together. They also found that volcanic dust, *pozzolana*, mixed with lime, water and rubble made an extremely strong concrete. This would harden anywhere, even under water.

Roman builders often used concrete for their arches, and as a core for their walls (see Figure d).

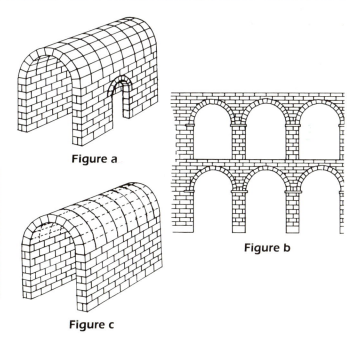

Figure a

Figure b

Figure c

SOURCE 4G Using the arch. These drawings show how Roman architects used the arch in single or combined form.

Figure d:
section of a wall, showing concrete core and triangular bricks.

47

Tools and machines

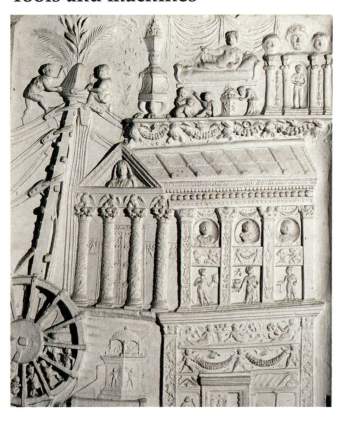

Many of the tools used by ancient craftsmen – chisels, hammers, planes, plumb-lines, squares and saws are very like our own. Cranes with treadmills and pulleys could lift heavy stone blocks to the top of a building. Water-powered saw-mills became common later.

4.11 Why was the arch so useful for Roman architects? *AT 1.3*

4.12 One material, not used by Roman builders, is found in most modern buildings. What is it, and what difference does it make to modern building design? *AT 1.3*

4.13 Why were carpenters so important in this kind of construction work? *AT 1.3*

4.14 Trajan's column is 39.8 metres high overall. How do you think the emperor's statue was put in place on the top? *AT 3.3*

SOURCE 4H Carving from a builder's tomb in Rome. It shows workmen putting a crane in position as they build a temple. When the crane had been firmly roped, the workmen used the treadmill and pulleys to hoist heavy weights to the top of the building.

Living in the capital

The fine buildings, monuments and open spaces made the centre of Rome very grand. The emperor's palace on the Palatine Hill had shaded garden walks and miniature lakes. On the slopes of the Esquiline Hill, north of the forums, were the fashionable mansions of many senators. But most of Rome was very overcrowded. A list of city buildings drawn up 200 years after Trajan's reign states that there were '1,790 private houses and 46,602 apartment blocks'.

This shows that most city-dwellers lived in rooms and flats. Some were built round a central courtyard, others simply opened onto a central staircase. They were often badly constructed, had no water and were always in danger from fire. Source 4I shows what one poet thought about Rome's accommodation.

Rome's streets

Carts were on the streets at night because vehicles were banned from the city during the day – unless they were builders' wagons 22 . For the ordinary Roman, it was as dangerous to be outside as to stay indoors, Source 4J.

SOURCE 4I

We live in a city held up by wooden props – that's how the landlords stop the apartments from falling down. They plaster over the cracks, and then tell the tenants to sleep tight – with the building balanced over them like a house of cards . . . then the fire starts . . . but you know nothing about it . . . the last to fry is the lodger in the loft!

Sick people die by the dozen through lack of sleep – you've got to be rich to afford the price of a snooze in Rome, with wagons rattling through the streets and their drivers cursing loudly enough to wake a walrus!

SOURCE 4J

The crowd blocks my way and the people behind tread on my heels. I get an elbow in the ribs . . . and a knock on the head from a plank or a barrel . . . everyone is treading on me . . . if a wagon turns over and sheds its load of stone all over the passers-by, what's left of their bodies? Who will identify the remains? . . . It's dangerous to go out at night. A tile from the roof can brain you, or a pot from an upstairs window . . . every open window is a deathtrap. Your friends will tell you that it's mad to go out to dinner without making a will!

4.15 These extracts come from a poem by Juvenal, who was writing in Trajan's times. His poems are called 'satires', and were written to criticise and make fun of the life of the city. Do some descriptions seem exaggerated to you? If so, which? Explain your answer. *AT 3.5*

4.16 If living in Rome was so dangerous, why did so many people choose to stay? *AT 1.4*

An apartment block at Ostia, Rome's harbour-town near the mouth of the river Tiber. Its upper storeys have disappeared, but it still helps us to work out what Rome's narrow streets looked like.

Keeping the people happy

Rome was a city of contrasts. Fine public buildings and squalid apartments stood side by side. Living conditions for the poor were cramped and dangerous; disease, violence and crime were very common. Emperors realised this, and tried to make life better for ordinary people by building magnificent baths, by providing water from the aqueducts and by offering grain at low prices. Above all, to give the city population something to look forward to, emperors put on expensive entertainments in the amphitheatre ◁18, the theatres and the Circus Maximus. Juvenal criticised this too:

SOURCE 4K

Long ago the ordinary people could hand out power, the fasces and military commands. Today they won't touch them – all they want is 'bread and games'.

4.17 What do you think that Juvenal meant when he wrote this? *AT 3.5 /2.3*

The Colosseum. Its great oval arena held about 50,000 spectators, who came to watch fighting and killing of every kind.

Races in the Circus Maximus

A four-horse chariot at full gallop. Notice how well protected the driver is.

You have already found out about the gladiatorial games ◁18 and the theatre ◁35. Most spectacular of all were the races in the Circus Maximus, which could hold 250,000 spectators – a quarter of the city's population. Each lap of the track was 1,100 metres (2 × 550), and most races were seven laps. Every turn was critical: if a driver swung too sharply, or collided, the chariot overturned. Slaves were stationed at the bends to clear injured bodies and shattered chariots off the track. A successful charioteer was a popular hero. This inscription records the career of Appuleius Diocles:

'. . . he started in 4,257 races and won 1,462 victories. . . . In total his prize-money was 8,965,780 denarii.'

4.18 Look at the wages and prices listed on page 69. What does this tell you about the rewards and dangers of being a charioteer? *AT 3.3*

Water supply – aqueducts and drains

Aqueducts

SOURCE 4L

Think how much water is needed for public buildings, baths, pools, private mansions, gardens and country houses close to the city. Then think how far the water has to travel before it reaches Rome.

Next, think about the aqueduct arches, the tunnels through the mountains and the level water channels across deep valleys – surely this is one of the world's most amazing achievements?

This is how the Elder Pliny describes the aqueduct built by the emperor Claudius in AD 38. It brought pure, cool water to Rome from the inland hills 68 kms away. By Trajan's time, about 1,000,000,000 litres per day were channelled to the city along nine aqueducts. The controller of the water supply, Julius Frontinus, was in charge of 420 kms of water channels. Here are some of the rules he made:

SOURCE 4M

A clear space must be left on both sides of water channels. No new buildings or tombs shall be allowed in these spaces; trees shall be cleared. The fine for each offence – 2,500 denarii.

No-one shall pierce or break the channel, pipes, tubes or public reservoirs, or stop the flow. Fine 25,000 denarii.

Arches from Claudius' aqueduct (the Aqua Claudia) still standing in the fields outside Rome. Some of the water for the modern city is still supplied by ancient aqueducts, repaired and carefully maintained over the centuries.

Individual householders could pay a large fee for a private supply from an aqueduct. But most inhabitants relied on tanks and public fountains at street corners.

Drains

Rome also had a drainage system to cope with all this water, and the city's liquid waste. The main drain, *Cloaca Maxima*, led from the Forum to an outlet into the river Tiber.

The opening of the Cloaca Maxima, where it emptied into the Tiber.

4.19 Write a short report called 'The Roman attitude to hygiene and sanitation', using the information in this chapter, from Britain 64▷ and from Pompeii. Give examples of Roman water technology and show how they used it. Find out what the drains and water-supply of a town near you were like 200 years ago and compare the standard. *AT 1.4*

4.20 Find out which reservoir your water supply comes from, and calculate the distance. *AT 1.4*

4.21 The Cloaca Maxima carried waste and rain water into the river Tiber. What are the drawbacks of this system? *AT 1.5*

4.22 In AD 90, a soldier earned 300 denarii each year. Comment on the fines set by Frontinus. *AT 1.6*

Centre of trade and travel

People from many different races and countries could always be seen on Rome's overcrowded streets.

SOURCE 4N

For years the rivers of the eastern empire have been pouring their filth into the Tiber, and bringing their languages, their strange habits and weird musical instruments to our Roman streets – not to mention the tarts who hang around the Circus.

Juvenal was not writing about real rivers, of course. He just wanted to show how much he disliked foreigners. But Rome was the centre of a great empire, and people from every province came to the capital. They brought their merchandise, fashions and foods, as well as their ideas and religious beliefs. It became safer to travel, by land and sea. Squadrons of warships (like the fleet commanded by the Elder Pliny) guarded the sea lanes, and the network of roads stretched throughout the whole empire. Britain became a province in AD 43: within 40 years almost 6,000 miles of roads had been built there. So traders and travellers from anywhere in the empire could set out for Rome knowing they had a good chance of arriving safely.

Read Source 4O to see what a Greek writer, Aelius Aristides, said about Rome and its empire in AD 150.

SOURCE 4O

It is now possible for anyone to travel wherever he wishes. The Greek poet Homer once said 'the earth is shared by all mankind', and Rome has made this come true. You Romans have measured every land in the civilized world; you have bridged rivers and cut through mountains for your highways . . .

From continents far and wide a constant flow of goods pours into Rome. From every land and every sea each season's crops come in . . . and articles skilfully made by Greek and foreign craftsmen. Merchants come from every direction: the city is the communal warehouse of the world. Everything comes here: anything that cannot be seen in Rome does not exist.

4.23 Compare Aristides' opinions with those of Juvenal. Whom do you believe and why?

AT
3.6
/2.7

4.24 In Source 4P pick out
   a) the lighthouse which Claudius built.
   b) the sea-god with his trident.
   c) the harbour buildings.

AT
3.3

4.25 Why should a harbour scene have so many gods on it? ◁7▷ The large eye is a protection against the Evil Eye.

SOURCE 4P   **This carving shows ships in the harbour at Ostia, Rome's port. One ship has just arrived, the other is moored. Most of the figures are gods.**

Centre of government

Along with goods and visitors, news and reports from the provinces reached Rome. They were brought by the imperial postal service, by officials returning home from overseas, by foreign ambassadors or even by merchants. The emperor and his governors in the provinces could send messages to each other surprisingly quickly. In AD 110 Trajan made the Younger Pliny governor of Bithynia and Pontus, far away on the southern shore of the Black Sea. Pliny's letters to the emperor and the emperor's replies tell us a great deal about the problems of running a province and an empire. Source 4Q opposite gives two examples.

> **SOURCE 4Q**
>
> **Pliny:** The bath-house at Prusa is old. The people will pay for a new one to be built if you give permission. . . .
>
> **Trajan:** Yes, provided that it does not strain the city's finances.
>
> **Pliny:** The citizens of Nicomedia have spent more than 3,500,000 sesterces towards the cost of aqueducts, but the projects were abandoned, and there is still no water-supply. . . .
>
> **Trajan:** The city must have a supply, but for goodness sake, find out who was to blame for all the money being wasted, and tell me who it was.

4.26 What sort of a governor was Pliny, and how good an emperor was Trajan, according to these extracts? *AT 3.3*

4.27 How reliable is the evidence in letters of this kind? *AT 3.7*

Persecuting the Christians

Pliny also wrote to Trajan to tell him how he was dealing with the Christians in his province:

> **SOURCE 4R**
>
> **Pliny:** . . . When people are charged with being Christians, I ask them face to face if this is true. If they admit it, I ask them twice more, and warn them about the punishment. If they still say they are Christians, I order them to be executed. . . . A nameless informer has also given me a list of suspected Christians. I order these suspects to pray to our gods, to offer wine and incense to your statue and to curse Christ. Anyone who does these things I set free – real Christians, I'm told, would never perform such actions . . . I also tried to find out the truth by torturing two slave women. They call them 'deaconesses'. . . .
>
> **Trajan:** You have acted correctly, Pliny. We cannot make fixed rules for dealing with Christians. But we must not hunt them down. Those who deny that they are Christians and pray to our gods must be pardoned, whatever they believed in the past. And have nothing to do with nameless informers. . . .

Emperor Trajan and his wife Plotina.

The Emperor Constantine

4.28 What do these extracts tell us about
a) the early Christians, their faith and the part played by women in the early church?
b) the attitudes of the Roman authorities to this new religion? *AT 3.3*

From Acts of the Apostles 1.15, describing events in about AD 30:

> **SOURCE 4S**
>
> Then they returned to Jerusalem from Mount Olivet. . . . and the number of the disciples was about 120.

Pliny writing to Trajan from Bithynia, AD 110:

> **SOURCE 4T**
>
> There are many people at risk from this superstition: men and women of all ages and every class are being brought to trial, from the towns, villages and countryside.

Eusebius, who wrote a History of the Christian church, described Constantine's vision before the battle he won to become emperor AD 312. In his dream, Constantine was told to paint the Christian emblem on his soldiers' shields, and to go into battle 'armed with this sign'. Constantine himself became a Christian just before he died in AD 337; soon Christianity was the official religion of the empire.

So 300 years passed between the first meetings of Jesus' disciples and Constantine's conversion to Christianity. For most of that time, people were suspicious of Christians and ready to persecute them. The first Christians therefore met in secret and used signs and passwords. Many Christians died as martyrs for their beliefs, but their numbers kept growing. Finally, in AD 313, Constantine passed a law allowing Christians to worship freely in public.

Two common Christian signs were:

1 The fish-shape. The Greek word for fish *ichthus* contains the first letters of the title 'Jesus Christ son of God, Saviour'.

2 The 'Chi-Rho' sign. 'Chi' and 'Rho' are both Greek letters – the first two in the name 'Christ'.

Underground cemetery (catacomb) outside Rome where the early Christians buried their dead. The catacombs were tunnelled secretly in the soft rock, so that Christians could be buried there without the authorities (or non-believers) knowing.

4.29 What helped Christianity to spread so fast? AT 1.5

4.30 Christians believe that there is only one true God. Why did this make them unpopular in Roman times? AT 1.3

4.31 Imagine how a fourth-century Christian felt on hearing that the emperor Constantine had become a Christian. Write a letter to another believer passing on the news and expressing your feelings. Remember that Christians could look back on hundreds of years of hiding and being hunted. AT 1.6

Living in the empire

The way Pliny treated the Christians in Bithynia seems cruel to us. But some Christian men and women suffered even more terribly in the persecutions of later emperors. Life in ancient times could be very harsh for those who were thought to be inferior or unusual in any way – slaves, for example, or war victims, those heavily in debt, the very poor and people who had peculiar beliefs. But most of the men and women who lived in the empire, especially during the second century AD, were grateful for 'the Roman peace' – *pax Romana* in Latin.

'Never forget, Romans,' wrote the poet Virgil, 'that your special skill will be to stamp your civilisation on a world at peace.' Roman armies guarded the frontiers, while Roman laws protected the rights of the people and kept order in the towns and cities.

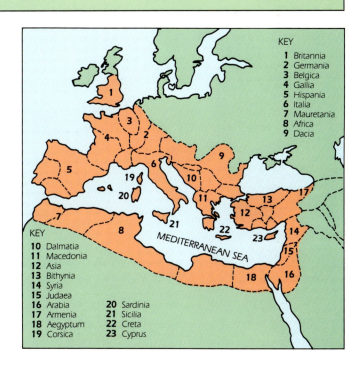

KEY
1 Britannia
2 Germania
3 Belgica
4 Gallia
5 Hispania
6 Italia
7 Mauretania
8 Africa
9 Dacia

KEY
10 Dalmatia
11 Macedonia
12 Asia
13 Bithynia
14 Syria
15 Judaea
16 Arabia
17 Armenia
18 Aegyptum
19 Corsica
20 Sardinia
21 Sicilia
22 Creta
23 Cyprus

MEDITERRANEAN SEA

SOURCE 4U **Map showing the Roman empire in the second century AD. The provinces are given their Latin names.**

Roman glass bottles from the 1st-2nd century AD. Goods like these would have been traded all over the empire.

SOURCE 4V The beautifully preserved temple in the forum at Nemasus, modern Nimes, in France.

Imagine a family, living somewhere in the empire – in Spain, or north Africa or on the coast of Asia Minor (modern Turkey) in AD 150. The town or city they lived in might be old – older than Rome itself

in the case of hundreds of Greek cities in the eastern Mediterranean – or a 'new town' built quite recently. The lives of all the family were affected by the empire. They could see around them the work of Roman architects and engineers: public baths, colonnades, new markets, basilicas, theatres, amphitheatres and aqueducts. Statues of emperors, past and present, stood in temples and public places, and many streets followed the Roman pattern. Local festivals were linked with celebrations in honour of Roman gods and emperors. Whatever their local language, the family's children would probably be educated in the Roman style, because this would improve their chances of a good career. When a boy or girl learned Latin they could make themselves understood anywhere in the western empire. If they learned Greek too they could talk to people throughout the Mediterranean. They could also read most of the world's great literature.

In schools everywhere, pupils read and memorised the writings of famous Greek and Latin authors. This histories of Livy ◁2 or Tacitus 58▷ , writings of Cicero ◁18 and the poetry of Virgil, Horace and Juvenal ◁48 could be bought cheaply in every city. Older students could have lessons from travelling scholars. These teachers brought new ideas from distant parts of the empire along its network of roads. Young men with talent and ambition often travelled to Rome to complete their education and become famous. Tacitus' family lived in southern Gaul, for example, and Suetonius came from north Africa. New religious beliefs travelled well too: St. Paul's journeys throughout Greece and Asia Minor are well known from the New Testament.

In local markets, people could buy goods from all over the empire and beyond. A rich lady in a north African villa could wear a dress of silk brought from China and spun at Tyre in Syria, with pearls from India; she could eat fresh figs from an elegant bowl made in Gaul, and sip Spanish wine from an Italian glass. She paid for all these items with coins which carried the portrait of the emperor and displayed his titles. These reminded people everywhere of the emperor's power and victories.

4.32 Use a modern atlas to find the present day equivalents of the Latin names in Source 4U, and make a separate list of all the ancient names that are still in use (e.g. Corsica).

AT 1.4

Coins and the historian

There were four main coins in the Roman money system.

1 aureus	= 25 denarii	= 100 sesterces	= 400 asses
(gold)	(silver)	(bronze)	(bronze)

It is very hard to tell accurately what a Roman coin is worth in modern money, but the coin itself gives useful information to historians. Designs were often changed because they provided excellent publicity.

Coins also helped people to know what their emperor looked like, or what he had been doing. A new coin was like a simple poster describing events.

4.33 On these coins find
- Judaea pictured as a sad female prisoner.
- One of Trajan's building projects.

4.34 Look at any coins you have. What can you learn from the pictures and writing on them? What will someone in AD 2050 be able to find out from them?

4.35 Look at some recent 'special issue' postage stamps. How does their message and design compare with the ancient coins?

Citizens of the empire

When St Paul returned to Jerusalem after his travels, Jews there began to riot. They hated his preaching and wanted him killed. Paul was arrested by the Roman garrison and chained up. This is what happened next, according to the story in the New Testament:

> **SOURCE 4W**
>
> The soldiers were going to whip Paul and question him. But he said to the centurion, 'Is it lawful for you to whip a Roman citizen?' When the centurion heard this, he asked his commanding officer:
> 'What are you going to do? This man is a Roman citizen'. . . . The commander was alarmed when he realized that Paul was a Roman citizen and that he had put him in chains.

For ordinary people, the greatest benefit of the empire was Roman citizenship. A citizen could go wherever he wished in the empire and be protected by law. Emperors gave citizen rights to individuals and to whole communities. By AD 200 almost every free person in the empire was a citizen. Citizens could also seek a career and promotion at Rome itself. Like Julius Caesar before him 22 , Emperor Claudius made some citizens from Gaul into Roman senators.

Here is an inscription from a small town in north Africa:

> **SOURCE 4X**
>
> To Quintus Lollius Urbicus, son of Marcus: this statue was set up by the town councillors. Lollius was a patron of the town, member of the road maintenance board, military tribune, quaestor in the Roman senate, and assistant to the governor of Asia, chosen as tribune and praetor by the emperor himself, commander of the 10th legion, served with emperor Hadrian on the Judaea campaign, priest, governor of Lower Germany and consul at Rome.

So Lollius, son of a wealthy family in a small African town, had a career which took him to Asia, Judaea, the river Danube (with the 10th legion), the Rhine, and on to be one of the most senior Roman magistrates. We shall see Lollius again 62▷ .

The emperor Hadrian, who promoted Lollius, was not born in Rome, or even in Italy. Like Trajan before him, his family came from Spain. Septimius Severus, emperor AD 193–211, came from north Africa. Rome ruled the provinces – but from AD 100 onwards, emperors from the provinces often ruled Rome.

4.36 Make two lists showing the benefits and disadvantages of living in one of Rome's provinces.

V ROMAN BRITAIN

The conquest of Britain

From the time of Julius Caesar's invasion ◁21 a stream of merchant ships sailed back and forth between Britain and the Roman empire. Many people in south-east England welcomed the goods and the ideas they brought, as Verica's coin (Source 5A) shows.

Then in AD 43 the emperor Claudius sent an army to invade Britain. He had been a sickly boy, crippled by polio, and had taken no part in public life. But by a strange chance he had been made emperor by the Praetorian Guard ◁25 . Now he needed to win the people's respect. Read Sources 5B, 5C and 5D which are quotations from Roman writers.

Two sides of a gold coin of Verica (Bericus) with a vine leaf (wine was imported from the Roman empire) and a Roman cavalryman. It shows that he welcomed Roman ideas.

SOURCE 5B

He thought the honours voted him by the senate were beneath his dignity, and wanted the glory of a proper triumph ◁21 . Britain seemed the best place to get one: no one else had tried to conquer it since Julius Caesar. Moreover the British kings were stirring up trouble because he had refused to send back to them some political refugees.

SOURCE 5C

About this time Aulus Plautius commanded an expedition to Britain. A man called Bericus [Verica] had been banished from the island after a political quarrel. He persuaded Claudius to send an army there, and Plautius was given command of it.

SOURCE 5D

Britain produces corn, cattle, gold, silver and iron. These are all exported, as well as leather, slaves and good hunting-dogs.
   The Britons are at least half a head taller than the tallest Romans, but bandy-legged and gawky.

5.1 For what reasons did Claudius invade Britain? Make a list of those you can think of, using the evidence in Sources 5B, 5C and 5D.

AT 3.3 /1.4

INVESTIGATIONS

Why did the Romans come to Britain?
What welcome did they get?
How far north did they go?
What benefits did they bring?

Key Sources
- Tacitus, Roman historian
- Roman remains that can still be seen – army camps, towns, villas, Hadrian's Wall

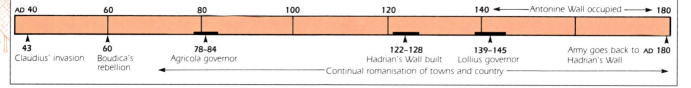

AD 40	60	80	100	120	140	←——Antonine Wall occupied——→ 180

43
Claudius' invasion

60
Boudica's rebellion

78–84
Agricola governor

122–128
Hadrian's Wall built

139–145
Lollius governor

Army goes back to AD 180
Hadrian's Wall

←———————— Continual romanisation of towns and country ————————→

The invasion

Aulus Plautius landed at Richborough with four legions. He conquered the British tribes one by one until he reached the place where the city of London was later built. British tribes had united to oppose him here, so Plautius waited.

> ### SOURCE 5E
>
> Guarding carefully the land he had won, he sent for Claudius. He had been ordered to do this if the opposition became too strong.
>
> Large reinforcements, including elephants, had already assembled. Claudius set out as soon as the message arrived. He sailed down the Tiber and round the coast to Marseilles. From there, he reached the Channel by road and river, sailed over, and joined the troops waiting at the Thames. He crossed the river, defeated the barbarians who had gathered to resist him, and captured Colchester.

5.2 Claudius was only in Britain for sixteen days. Why do you think he was so successful so quickly? *AT 1.3*

5.3 Claudius was away from Rome for six months. What does this tell you about his journeys between Marseilles and the Channel? *AT 1.3*

One of the legionary commanders, who later became the emperor Vespasian, captured 20 hill forts like this one in Dorset, known as Maiden Castle.

In four years Aulus Plautius occupied the south-eastern part of Britain. Claudius probably thought that this new province was now big enough. To mark its frontier Plautius built the Fosse Way, a road from Lincoln to Exeter. But the Britons outside the province continued to attack it. So the Roman army gradually advanced into Wales, building forts to hold down the obstinate tribes.

The last battle was for the island of Anglesey. In AD 60 the Roman commander, Suetonius Paulinus, captured it. The fighting seemed to be over, but dreadful news came.

Rebellion

King Prasutagus of the Iceni had just died. He left some of his property to the emperor, but Roman officials wanted to take over the whole kingdom. When his widow, Queen Boudica, protested, she was flogged and her daughters raped. The British tribes rebelled in fury.

> ### SOURCE 5F
>
> In particular the Britons hated the ex-soldiers who had been settled in Colchester. These men robbed the Britons of their houses and land, and called them 'prisoners' and 'slaves'. Moreover, the temple built for the emperor Claudius showed that the Romans were never going to leave.

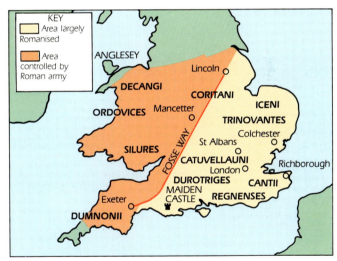

The area occupied by the Romans by AD 60. The names of the various British kingdoms are in capitals.

Boudica and her army butchered every Roman in Colchester. Crushing a Roman legion that tried to stop them, they took their revenge, looting and burning as they went. St Albans was destroyed, then London. Over 70,000 Romans died. 'The Britons hanged them, crucified them, cut their throats or burnt them at the stake.'

A model of the Temple of Claudius built at Colchester. Its extensive vaulted foundations can be seen today, and many pieces of burnt marble from its superstructure have been found.

But Suetonius had been given time to gather a large army. Somewhere near Mancetter (in Warwickshire) they slaughtered the enemy, killing over 80,000 Britons. Boudica committed suicide.

This skull, savagely hacked by swords, was found in a war grave at Maiden Castle.

5.4 What causes have you read here for Boudica's revolt? Can you think of other possible reasons for it?
AT 1.4 /3.3

5.5 Imagine you are Boudica. Make up a speech for her to deliver to her people, telling them why it is right to treat the Romans so savagely.
AT 1.6

Revenge and rebuilding

After defeating Boudica, Suetonius and his men thought of nothing but taking their revenge. They could not forget the burned and tortured corpses of the women and children in the three sacked cities. Feelings were so strong that fighting raged for over a year.

SOURCE 5G

Every tribe which had rebelled, or had been unreliable, was battered down by fire or sword. But the greatest hardship for the Britons was famine. They had conscripted their men, young and old, for the war, and had not bothered to sow crops, expecting to use Roman supplies instead.

This is the report of Tacitus, the Roman historian. He had married the daughter of Agricola, governor of Britain from AD 78–84 [62]▷ and probably heard a lot from him about the wars in Britain.

But one man urged Suetonius to forget the past, and to work for peace. He was Julius Classicianus, a financial officer. Tacitus wrote:

SOURCE 5H

The Britons were stubborn and too slow to accept peace, because Julius Classicianus advised them to wait for the next governor, who would treat them more mercifully if they surrendered. He told them that the new governor would be free from anger or pride since he had not fought or defeated them. At the same time Classicianus reported to Rome that there was no hope for an end of fighting unless Suetonius was replaced.

5.6 Can you blame Suetonius for hating the Britons? Explain your answer.
AT 1.3

5.7 Who in Rome would read Classicianus' report?
AT 1.1

Classicianus

Classicianus is not just a name to us. He died in Britain, and was buried in London. Most of his tombstone was discovered in 1935, and it is now in the British Museum. From the inscription we can see that he was born in the province of Gaul, and that his family was probably given Roman citizenship by Augustus. His wife's father was Julius Indus, well known at the time: he had formed a cavalry regiment, which became part of the garrison of Britain.

So Classicianus was a member of a new class of provincial aristocrats. These were well-educated, capable men, born in the provinces, not in Rome ◁ 55 . More and more of them began to work for the emperor in the administration of the provinces.

5.8 Say in your own words what you think 'the administration of the provinces' means. AT 1.4

5.9 Why did the emperors want men born in the provinces to do this sort of work in the provinces? AT 1.3

Roads and romanisation

The emperor Nero agreed with Classicianus and recalled Suetonius. Nero thought that if the province was good to live in, the people would not want to rebel. He ordered the building of new towns and roads, and encouraged the people to adopt Roman ideas and customs. We call this 'romanisation'. There had been no roads, only a few tracks worn by the feet of travellers. Now proper roads would allow the soldiers to get about wherever they were needed. Ordinary people and merchants could also travel easily, and this would help trade.

This road at Blackstone Edge, in West Yorkshire, ran down a hill. The groove in the large blocks of stone in the centre was worn by the brake-poles of wagons coming carefully down the slope.

Making roads

To find the line of a road, surveyors took sights from one high point to the next. In flat and wooded country they looked for the smoke from fires lit by their men. They chose the shortest, straightest route, only making corners if they had no choice. Roman roads are long and straight, with bends on the high points where the sightings were taken. Marching men preferred a short steep climb to trudging round a long hill.

Labourers cleared the trees or turf, then dug a ditch about a metre deep to take the big foundation stones which they rammed down into it. Often, instead of a ditch, they piled up earth from the drainage ditches into a wide embankment, and set the stones in this. Next came smaller stones, followed by layers of sand, clay or gravel. Then for the surface, slabs of stone were laid, or anything else suitable that could be found nearby. In the Weald of Kent, for example, the slag from iron mines was used, and this rusted into an incredibly hard surface.

5.10 Why is there a curve, or camber, on the surface? AT 1.3

5.11 What other purpose might the ditches have apart from drainage? AT 1.3

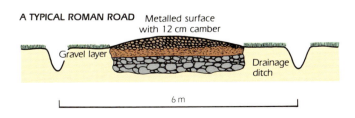

A TYPICAL ROMAN ROAD Metalled surface with 12 cm camber
Gravel layer
Drainage ditch
6 m

SOURCE 5I How a road was built (where no embankment was needed).

Roman towns with English names

Aquae Sulis	Bath
Calleva	Silchester
Camulodunum	Colchester
Corinium	Cirencester
Deva	Chester
Durovernum	Canterbury
Durnovaria	Dorchester
Eburacum	York
Glevum	Gloucester
Isca Silurum	Caerleon
Isca Dumnoniorum	Exeter
Isurium	Aldborough
LINdum COLoNia	Lincoln
Petuaria	Brough
Magna	Kenchester
Noviogmagus	Chichester
Ratae	Leicester
Venta Belgarum	Winchester
Venta Icenorum	Caistor St. Edmunds
Venta Silurum	Caerwent
Verulamium	St. Albans
Viroconium	Wroxeter

Many of these English names come from the Latin word *castra*, military camp.

These are the most important roads and towns of Roman Britain.

New towns

Before the Romans came, forests covered much of Britain. Most people were farmers; some lived by hunting. Everybody lived in round thatched huts, which they shared with their sheep, cows, pigs and chickens.

The Britons were used to living in tribes, under tribal kings. The Romans did not try to change this. But the Romans liked good towns, with law-courts, shops, market places and tax offices. So they helped the kings to build towns, and made the kings feel important by making them governors of the towns and the countryside round about.

Towns were built for 14 of the biggest tribes. The Romans planned the towns and provided the money while, just as in road-building, the Britons provided the labourers. Surveyors, foremen and skilled craftsmen came from the legions.

5.12 Why did the Romans keep the kings in command of their tribes? `AT 1.3`

5.13 Towns were built because they were useful, and because the Romans believed that life in towns was better for everyone. Do you agree? Give your reasons. `AT 1.3`

The network of roads eventually reached all over the country. Many of our modern towns have developed from Roman towns. Since Roman surveyors chose the best routes for the roads that linked them, these routes have been used ever since. However you can rarely see the Roman roads today, for railways, main roads or motorways have covered them.

Into Scotland

After ten years of 'romanisation' a new emperor, Vespasian , ordered the army in Britain to push northwards again. By AD 78 most of England had been conquered. Then a new governor came, Gnaius Julius Agricola. In the biography of Agricola, Tacitus says that in seven years he occupied most of the rest of Britain, as the map shows. The final battle was fought at Curno, in Grampian. Tacitus quotes the British commander's view of the Romans:

'For robbery, murder and looting they use the lying word *empire*, and when they have made a wasteland, they call it peace.'

5.14 Do you think the British commander really spoke those words? Why does Tacitus quote them? *AT 3.5*

This is Tacitus' description of the scene after the battle:

SOURCE 5J

The Britons scattered, men and women weeping together as they dragged away the wounded and called to the survivors. Many of them abandoned their homes, and even set them on fire in their anger, then chose hiding-places but immediately left them. They gathered to make some sort of plan, but then broke up again. Sometimes their hearts were broken by the sight of their loved ones, more often it drove them to frenzy; we found out that some of them even killed their wives and children in a kind of pity.

On the next day it was easier to see what victory looked like. There was an awful silence everywhere. The hills were deserted; in the distance smoke rose from their houses.

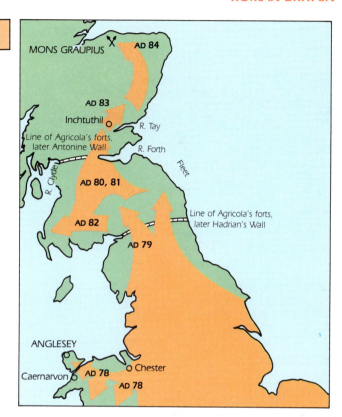

Agricola's advances, and the position of Hadrian's wall.

5.15 What does this quotation tell you about the feelings of Tacitus and Agricola towards the Britons and the Roman campaigns? *AT 3.3*

When Agricola left Britain, Tacitus lost interest in it. At some time the army moved back to a line of forts which Agricola had built, between the rivers Tyne and Solway. And there the army stayed. In AD 122 the emperor Hadrian visited Britain and decided that the Romans should give up trying to conquer Scotland and that the legions must build a permanent frontier. We know it as Hadrian's Wall.

Hadrian's Wall

This massive stone wall crossed England from Carlisle to Newcastle. It took the legions six years to build and was between 2.5 and 3.5 metres thick, and nearly 5 metres high. Soldiers could walk along the top, protected by a parapet about 1.5 metres high which faced north. There was a ditch on the north side of the wall. Along the wall were 79 milecastles, each holding about 50 men: two signal towers were set between all the milecastles. At roughly equal intervals there were 16 large forts, intended for 1,000 infantrymen, or 500 cavalry. There were about 9,500 men stationed along the wall, all auxiliary, or non-Roman, troops.

Part of Hadrian's Wall today, with the remains of a milecastle.

5.16 What was the purpose of the wall? Why was it necessary? `AT 1.3`

5.17 Why did the forts hold 500 cavalrymen but 1,000 foot-soldiers? `AT 1.3`

5.18 Imagine that you are a soldier serving in one of the forts, or his girl-friend. Write home to your mother in Gaul, telling her what your life is like. `AT 1.6`

This latrine in the fort at Housesteads has small gullies and basins where the soldiers washed their hands and the sponges they used instead of toilet paper.

Lollius comes to Britain

Quintus Lollius Urbicus ◁55 came to govern Britain in AD 139. He had been ordered by the new emperor to conquer the people beyond Hadrian's Wall and build another wall in Scotland. He needed the legions for this and we can be sure that Lollius visited the great legionary fortresses at Caerleon, Chester and York.

Army camps

The Jewish priest called Josephus ◁46 , who had fought the Roman army in the Jewish rebellion of AD 66–70, wrote this:

SOURCE 5L   **A model of the legionary fortress at Chester: it covered nearly 50 acres (a football pitch covers one acre).**

> SOURCE 5K
>
> *They never let the enemy catch them unawares. In enemy country they always build a camp before fighting a battle. They make the ground level if it is uneven, and mark out a square for the camp. To build it the army takes along a great number of tools and workmen.*
>
> *The interior is divided into rows of tents, and outside there are towers at regular intervals along the perimeter, which looks just like a wall. A gate is built into each of the four sides, to provide an easy entrance for the baggage animals, and wide enough for the troops to dash out quickly if there is an emergency . . .*
>
> *The camp is conveniently divided into four quarters by streets: the officers' quarters are in the middle, with the general's headquarters in the exact centre. And so it is very like a city, with its market place, the craftsmen's section, and the offices where tribunes and centurions settle the men's quarrels.*
>
> *The outer wall, and the buildings inside, are completed very quickly. If necessary they dig a ditch outside the wall, two metres deep and two metres wide.*

When the legions stayed anywhere for a long time, these temporary camps were turned into permanent fortresses. Wooden huts replaced the tents, and in time stone replaced wood.

5.19 These camps were always laid out in the same pattern. Why do you think this was so? `AT 1.3`

5.20 How well does the picture of the camp in Source 5L match Josephus' description? `AT 3.4`

Town Planning

The first town had been built at Colchester in AD 49, as a home for retired soldiers. When Boudica's army destroyed it, Colchester already had a temple, a 'senate-house' where the local council met, and a theatre.

5.21 Stone and marble from Claudius' temple have been found in Colchester. But we only know of the senate-house and theatre because a historian mentions them: what materials do you think they were made of? `AT 1.3`

Archaeologists have found that Colchester had its streets at right angles, and its most important buildings at the centre. So did any town where legions had been stationed, or which the Romans helped the British tribes to build. This is not surprising, because the architects and planners came from the legions, and it is a sensible design. The rectangular areas in this right-angled grid of streets were known as *insulae*, islands. In these insulae were the public buildings, shops and private houses.

All these towns are marked on the map on page 60.

Towns that just grew

Not all the towns were built with Roman help. Many grew where main roads crossed, for example, and inns, shops and stables were built to serve travellers. Sometimes buildings arose around small army forts, where the soldiers' families lived. Often when the troops moved away, the civilian settlement was big enough to survive without the soldiers and developed into a town. In these towns the streets were not usually laid out in the right-angled grid pattern.

5.22 Why do you think these towns were not built in the regular pattern?

This plan was made after the excavators finished in AD 1909. The blank spaces in the insulae were probably occupied by wooden buildings. Archaeologists at that time could not recognise the signs left in soil by wooden buildings which had rotted away.

An aerial photograph of another Roman town, Silchester. It was built as the capital town of a Celtic tribe, the Atrebates. Because the soil over the roads is thinner, the grass grows a different colour.

© Crown copyright 1991/MOD.

Living in towns

As he went north Lollius would have been accompanied by his wife. They passed through many towns. None were very old, and some were still being built. Some streets were unpaved and muddy, others were cobbled, or paved with stone slabs. Town houses in Britain were not like those at Pompeii . Most were long, narrow houses, of four or five rooms with the shorter end on the street. Older houses were built entirely of wood.

5.23 Why do you think British town houses were different from those in Pompeii?

As Britain grew richer, new stone houses, with one or two storeys, replaced the wooden ones. Some were larger, built round a courtyard or garden.

This picture was taken while a Roman town house was being excavated at Colchester. What parts of it can you see?

Painted plaster from a house at St Albans. What pictures has the painter used to decorate it?

At first the floors were of hard beaten earth, perhaps covered with straw. Later, concrete was laid and sometimes small coloured pieces of stone were set into the wet cement. Some of these 'mosaics' can still be seen where they were laid, but some are in museums.

5.24 What do we use today instead of mosaics for decorating floors? What are the advantages and disadvantages of mosaics? `AT 1.3`

These floors were very cold. Heating came from open fires on stone hearths or in iron baskets. Some houses also had the *hypocaust*, a form of underfloor heating ◁34 .

Shops

As Lollius and his wife approached the middle of a town they saw all sorts of shops. They were like houses, but the end wall was replaced by shutters. During the day they were open to the street, and goods for sale were on display, or being made. Just as at Pompeii, the owner and his family lived behind these rooms or above the shop. Nowadays, when foundations are being dug for modern buildings, the remains of old Roman houses and shops are sometimes uncovered. Wine jars, carpenters' tools, perfume bottles, meat bones, pottery bowls and pots and pans, leather-goods and pieces of woven cloth have been found in some of these and show what sort of shops there were.

5.25 Roman shops usually sold a much narrower range of goods than shops today. Discuss the reasons in your groups. `AT 1.3`

Water

At least one of the insulae contained a public bath-house and lavatory. The baths were very like those in Pompeii ◁33 . Large towns had several bath-houses. They used great quantities of water, which was fed into the town from nearby springs and streams by *aqueducts;* these were usually pipes made from earthenware, lead or wood. Aqueducts were not very long in Britain, and rarely had to be carried on stone arches. The town-council had to provide a water supply and keep it in good condition. Some private houses may have drawn water from the public aqueducts, but most had their own wells.

All the water from the bath-houses, lavatories and private houses, as well as rain water, had to be drained away, and most towns had underground drains and sewers, sometimes made of wood, but more often of stone or brickwork. These carried the water into nearby rivers.

Cursus Publicus – the public post

Official messages were carried by messengers who would also carry private messages for important people. They travelled in a carriage, and frequently changed horses at staging posts every twelve to fifteen miles along the roads or in every town. The post carriages and horses could be used by officials, and sometimes private travellers who were given a travelling passport, or *diploma*, by the emperor or a provincial governor.

Seventy to one hundred miles a day was considered fast. When the emperor Tiberius travelled 200 miles in 24 hours to reach his sick brother in Germany, Pliny called it 'a wonderful thing, and an example of incredible speed'.

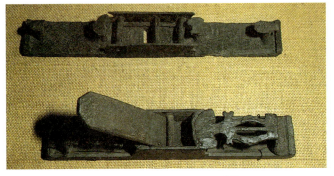

What were these Roman carpentry tools?

Where to stay

Every town had a guest house, *mansio*, for travelling officials which was maintained at the state's expense. It sometimes occupied a whole *insula*. The managers made sure that the water in the mansio baths was hot, food was ready and fresh horses were waiting for the next stage of the journey. Some travellers in Lollius' group were not officials and had to find lodgings in an inn. These had a reputation for being dirty and dangerous and their visitors were often robbed.

5.26 *Why was a quick postal service important in running the empire?*

The forum

Lollius and his party went on to the forum in the middle of the town, where the town officials, local aristocrats and dignitaries had gathered to meet them.

As usual it had a large open court where people could stroll and talk, and where traders would erect their stalls, just as in market squares today. The court was surrounded on three sides by shops and offices. On the fourth side was the *basilica*, the equivalent of a modern town hall. This large hall was normally used for meetings of the town council. Along the side of the hall was a row of offices, for the lawyers, tax-collectors, town surveyors and council clerks.

The council was made up of the 100 richest citizens. Every year they chose four officials, two in charge of the law-courts, and to make sure that the taxes were collected, and two to look after the streets, markets, public buildings and water supply. These four were granted Roman citizenship.

Men like these were anxious to meet Lollius, because he was important and famous. They wanted to find out how this new governor would treat them. Lollius could discover whether the Britons were likely to oppose him or help his ideas for the province.

5.27 *What would happen to the population of a town if four of its most important people were granted Roman citizenship every year?* AT 1.4

Religion

Lollius was amazed by the temples which he saw in the towns. These were not like the classical temple of Claudius at Colchester ◁58 , but were tall buildings surrounded by a verandah. They were Celtic temples, for Celtic gods. But the Romans worshipped these gods as well as the Britons, believing that any god might help them. The Romans also brought their own gods to Britain, like Jupiter and Diana, Mars and Venus ◁8 , or Mithras, the soldier's god, and some of the Britons chose to worship them as well.

A Celtic temple.

Entertainment

On his way out of town Lollius saw an amphitheatre. Here shows like gladiator-fights ◁18 , circus acts, bull fights, bear-baiting, cockfighting, boxing or wrestling were put on. The town officials were expected to arrange and pay for some of these. Travelling entertainers would also hire the amphitheatre, hoping to make profit. Many towns had amphitheatres, but only four in Roman Britain had theatres, and these were used for religious ceremonies more often than for the sort of plays we see in our theatres.

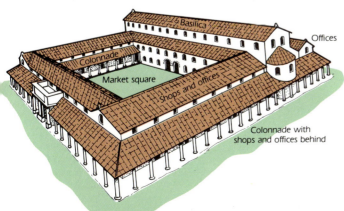

This picture shows what the forum of the Roman town Viroconium (Wroxeter) was like. Nearly all the other 14 tribal capitals had similar forums.

© Crown copyright 1991/MOD.

The Roman theatre at St Albans, as it is today.

65

Population

There were about eighty settlements in Roman Britain which can be called towns. London was the largest, with perhaps 30,000 inhabitants. It covered 330 acres, and was the second largest town north of the Alps. The smallest towns covered only four or five acres, and under 1,000 people lived in them.

In Britain there were about 100,000 Roman soldiers and a few thousand Roman traders and officials. All the rest were Britons. When Agricola was governor he praised the Britons' intelligence, and told his son-in-law Tacitus:

> **SOURCE 5M**
>
> *Men who a short time before refused to learn Latin now wanted to speak it fluently. Roman fashions were popular, and the toga could often be seen. Gradually the Britons sank to the attractive bad habits of colonnades, bath-houses and elegant dinner parties. These simple people called it 'civilisation': really it was only one way of keeping them quiet.*

Though many Britons learnt Latin, which was the official language of the empire, they also continued to speak their native Celtic languages.

5.28 Men and women went to shop, or stroll and chat in colonnades: why is this an 'attractive bad habit'? `AT 1.3`

5.29 What does Tacitus mean by saying 'the toga could often be seen'?

5.30 Do you agree with the last sentence of what Tacitus said? `AT 2.3`

One man's beliefs

Once, a centurion of the 2nd Legion put up four dedication stones side by side; they were:

1 to Jupiter

2 to Apollo and Diana

3 to Mars, Minerva, Epona (a Celtic horse god) and Victory

4 to 'The Spirit of the Land of Britain'.

5.31 Why did the centurion respect so many gods? `AT 1.6`

5.32 Do you think he believed in all of them? `AT 1.6`

The countryside

As Lollius's party travelled north they saw busy farms by the side of the roads. Many people in the new towns no longer worked on the land. They bought their food instead of growing it. The soldiers also needed meat, leather and wool. The troops ate corn as well, but this had to be supplied free as a tax. So local farmers had cut down forests and planted more corn or reared more sheep and cattle. They learnt new techniques from the Romans and with better ploughs and drainage they cultivated more land. They dried their corn over hypocausts, and could keep it from one year to the next.

Farmers, especially in the south-east, became prosperous. They could afford Italian or Spanish wine, and better tools. Their wives bought new designs of pottery and tableware imported from the continent. New crops, like apples, plums, cherries, flax, rye, carrots and cabbage were planted. People were healthier with this varied diet and cleaner water, and lived longer.

Villas

Most of the farmhouses were still round thatched huts. But some rich farmers built splendid farmhouses called *villas*. These were much more like modern houses, with square rooms, plastered walls and a tiled roof.

Villas like this one were built all over northern Europe. This picture is based on the excavation of Gorhambury Roman villa.

5.33 Most villas were near towns and roads: why do you think this was so? `AT 1.3`

5.34 The villa owners were Britons, not Romans. How do you think they found out about the villa style of farm-house? `AT 1.3`

Some of the new villas were big and elegant. One at Bignor, in Sussex, had many rooms with mosaic floors, and *two* bath-houses, one for the owner and his family, and another for the estate-workers. The estate covered over 2,000 acres. But pig-sties, barns and cattlesheds were as important as bath-houses and elegant rooms, for the villas were still working farmhouses from which the owner made his living. Most of them are in the south-east of Britain, which was the wealthiest part of the province, and over 700 have been found.

Industry in the countryside

Not all the workers in the countryside were farmers. There was a gold mine at Dolaucothi in Wales and an aqueduct six miles long brought water to wash the ore. Iron, lead (from which silver could be extracted), tin and copper, were mined. There were bunkers full of coal in some of the forts of Hadrian's wall. Coal was dug from surface quarries as there were no deep mines. Stone quarries produced millstones and whetstones as well as

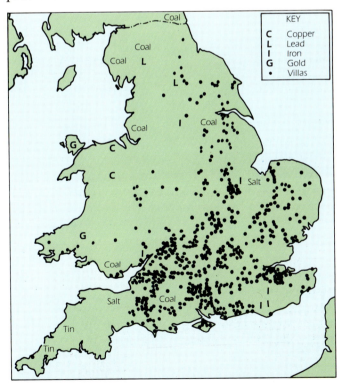

The dots indicate where villas have been excavated. There must be many which have not been discovered. You can see where minerals were mined. In which places are the same minerals still mined today?

blocks for building. Pearls were found off the coast at Whitstable. Jet, from Whitby in Yorkshire was carved into beads and necklaces, and shale, a soft soapy stone found in Dorset, was worked into cups, table-legs and trays.

5.35 We have no written information about all these products: how do you think we know about them? `AT 3.2`

5.36 What do you think are the biggest differences between modern industry and industry in Roman Britain and the ancient world? `AT 1.4`

Vindolanda

When Lollius reached Hadrian's Wall he saw the little towns and villages which had quickly grown up round the camps and milecastles. The soldiers' families lived in them, and the shopkeepers or bathhouse-keepers who looked after the soldiers.

One of these civilian settlements, known as Vindolanda, has been excavated recently and coins and jewels, gold rings and brooches, have been found. There are also over 200 fragments of wooden writing tablets. Writing can be seen, though the letters are tiny, and the writing is often careless.

One was a letter recommending a young officer to the commandant of the fort. Another was to a young soldier telling him that he would receive a parcel containing some woollen socks, two pairs of sandals and two pairs of underpants. Another document covers eight days in June. It lists the payments made into the regimental strong-room (for soldiers' savings?). It also records the quantities issued of barley, corn, fish-sauce, pork-fat, spices, salt, vintage wine and sour wine (the soldiers' normal drink), beer, goat's meat, young pig, ham and venison.

5.37 Why do you think records like this were kept? What do they tell us about life on Hadrian's wall? `AT 1.3`

5.38 Collect information from Chapters 4 and 5 and prepare a debate on the question 'What did the Britons owe the Romans?' `AT 3.4`

The Antonine Wall

Lollius did succeed in pushing the frontier into Scotland. He built the Antonine Wall, named after the emperor Antoninus. But within 40 years it was abandoned, and Hadrian's Wall remained the northern frontier of the empire for another 250 years.

VI END OF EMPIRE

Defending Britain

In AD 196 Clodius Albinus, governor of Britain, took the legions across the Channel in an attempt to become emperor. Septimius Severus, the existing emperor, quickly defeated Albinus. But while Albinus was in Gaul, wild Scottish tribes seized the chance and swept south, killing and looting. They destroyed much of Hadrian's Wall. Severus sent a new governor to recover the province. In AD 208 Severus himself arrived, and punished the northerners so harshly that there was peace for 60 years. Severus died in York in AD 211.

Septimis Severus AD 193–211.

6.1 A Roman emperor spent three years in Britain. What does this tell you about the importance of Britain in the empire? AT 1.3

The rest of the empire had a troubled century . Though the Britons had to pay their taxes, they escaped the plague, and the barbarian hordes which ravaged the continent. But from about AD 275 to 285 Britain *was* in danger: pirate fleets of Franks and Saxons, from north Germany, raided our coasts. Sidonius Apollinaris, a Christian bishop, describes them in Source 6A.

SOURCE 6A

They are the most savage enemies. They beat aside all resistance, and butcher anyone they catch unawares. No ship can outsail them. They are not afraid of shipwreck, but welcome it as useful experience! In stormy weather landsmen think they cannot be attacked: but the Saxons cannot be seen, and dash in through rock and wave.

Before they make for home, they drown or hang one in ten of their captives. They do this for religious reasons, which makes it all the more horrifying.

To resist these pirates, stone walls were put round many British towns. Great fortresses were built along the coasts of Britain and France. Spring-loaded guns were set on bastions, the great round towers attached to their walls, which we can still see. Ships were kept ready to sail out against the invaders. With this protection, Britain became peaceful again.

The walls and bastions of the fort at Porchester overlooking Portsmouth harbour. The church and castle were built much later.

INVESTIGATIONS

How Britain fared as the empire collapsed
How the empire ended
What the Christian Church did
What survived the end of empire

Key Sources
- Ancient historians
- Roman defence works in Britain
- Modern languages, law and medicine
- Architecture, ancient and modern

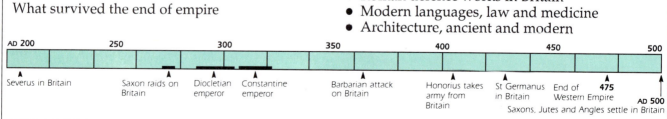

Re-organising the empire

A tough soldier called Diocletian ◁26 seized power in AD 284, and slowly restored order to the empire. He turned it into a military state. He made the army more important than anything else, and the soldiers became the privileged class. He split the empire into four parts: Diocletian and his Caesar ◁25 ruled the richer eastern parts, and fellow- soldiers were the Augustus and Caesar of the western parts.

6.2 Why did Diocletian treat the army so well?

AT 1.3

The portrait on this coin emphasises Diocletian's tough character.

'The Tetrarchs': this statue group clearly expresses the 'togetherness' of the two Augusti and two Caesars.

Extracts from Diocletian's lists

SOURCE 6B

Wages:

Sewer-cleaner, shepherd	per day	20 denarii
Carpenter, baker, shipwright	per day	50 denarii
Tailor, for cutting a pair of breeches		20 denarii
Teacher of arithmetic, per boy, per month		75 denarii
Advocate, fee for pleading one case		1,000 denarii

Goods:

Boots, farmworker's, without hobnails		120 denarii
Cleaned rice	per litre	20 denarii
Honey, best quality	per litre	64 denarii
Butter	per pound	16 denarii
Beef	per pound	12 denarii
One chicken		30 denarii
Refined gold	per pound	50,000 denarii
White silk	per pound	12,000 denarii
Raw silk, dyed purple	per pound	150,000 denarii

Control of prices and wages

To ordinary people the greatest hardship was price rises. Diocletian published lists of maximum prices and wages. But so many people now worked in the army or civil service, instead of industry or agriculture, that food and other goods ran short. Price controls were abandoned, but wages were still fixed. The army of civil servants enforcing the regulations was nearly as large as the army of soldiers. Taxes were put up to pay for them. A census was taken every five years, to make sure that no one escaped the tax-collectors. People were forbidden to move about the country while the census was being taken. Later they had to stay for all their lives where the census-takers found them.

6.3 The annual pay of a soldier was 300 denarii in AD 90, and 750 denarii in AD 210. If we think of a soldier earning much the same as a craftsman (who worked about 250 days a year), roughly how many denarii did one of Diocletian's soldiers earn?

AT 3.1

6.4 How many days did a shepherd have to work to buy a pair of boots? Would a farm-worker today have to work as long?

AT 3.3

6.5 Compare Roman wages and food prices. Is food today, compared with modern wages, cheaper or dearer? Why do you think this is so?

AT 3.3 /1.2

Between AD 300 and AD 400 prices multiplied another 45 times!

Constantine and his city

In AD 305 **four** rival Augusti appeared. One was Constantine: he was at York when his soldiers declared him Augustus. He believed that Diocletian had been wrong to divide the empire. Over the years he fought and defeated his rivals. He became sole emperor in AD 323.

Constantine saw that the western half of his empire was poor and troubled. The eastern half was rich and growing richer: its neighbours were not barbarians, but civilised people, trading in luxury goods from China and India. The old Greek city of Byzantium would be a better place for the capital of the empire, more convenient for controlling the frontiers along the Rhine, Danube and Euphrates. It also had a superb, easily-defended, harbour, ideal for trade. So Constantine transferred the capital there, and from AD 330 to 340 built a new city, named Constantinople – 'City of Constantine'. It became the capital of the eastern empire when the empire was divided again in AD 364.

6.6 Constantine probably united the empire so that the richer eastern half could help to defend the west. What would have happened if he had not done so?

6.7 What would you expect to happen when the halves were separated?

Prosperity in Britain

Life in Britain at this time probably seemed better than anywhere else in the empire. British industries flourished and home products replaced imports. The tin mines in Cornwall were re-opened, and British tin was now sold all over the empire. It was often mixed with lead to form pewter, and pewter tableware became common.

Surplus British corn was sold to the continent. British woollen goods were popular, and British duffle-coats and travelling rugs were mentioned in Diocletian's price list. Grapes were now grown in British vineyards. The drinking vessels of this time which have been excavated often contained about 1.5 litres; it seems that beer was becoming more popular than wine: British beer was in the price list at 4 denarii per pint.

The most obvious sign of wealth is seen in the towns and villas. The theatre at Verulamium was enlarged. The basilica at Silchester was completely rebuilt, and the bath-houses here and at Canterbury were rebuilt to new designs. In the countryside archaeologists have uncovered around 70 really magnificent villas built in this time, with fine mosaics and extensive hypocaust systems. The villa at Chedworth replaced a much smaller earlier villa. In addition to living rooms it had workshops reserved for craftsmen like blacksmiths, potters and fullers. Most of these great villas were probably built by rich men from other parts of the empire, looking for a safe and pleasant place to live.

6.8 Why do you think Britain was better off than the rest of Europe? _AT 1.3_

6.9 How would these rich immigrants have benefitted the Britons? _AT 1.3_

Britain attacked

Eventually Britain's wealth proved too tempting. In AD 367 all the barbarians – Scots (from Ireland), Picts (from Scotland), Franks and Saxons – conspired together: their synchronised attacks were devastating. The Wall was overrun and its forts and civil settlements destroyed. Most of the towns survived, but the villas, even in the south, suffered enormous damage. The whole province was in chaos.

Theodosius, one of Rome's greatest generals, was sent to win Britain back. He landed at Richborough and, according to the historian Ammianus Marcellinus:

> **SOURCE 6C**
>
> With four legions he set out for London. He attacked the enemy bands, still wandering about in search of booty, and weighed down with their plunder. He quickly overcame those who were driving along cattle and chained captives, and stripped them of the loot which they had taken from the unfortunate provincials. He handed it all back to the provincials except for a small part which he gave to his weary soldiers.

Theodosius drove out all the barbarians in the end. The forts along Hadrian's Wall were clumsily repaired, and men, women and children all lived inside them. Bastions for spring-loaded artillery, like those of the Forts of the Saxon Shore, were added to the walls of many towns. The province was now on the defensive. If the barbarian raids could not be prevented, at the first sign of danger everyone was to flock into the towns, and wait till the raiders departed. The system worked: prosperity returned and lasted until nearly the end of the century.

An aerial view of Chedworth Villa: the large modern house occupies the site of the original front gateway.

Barbarians and Byzantium

Life was grim in the rest of the western empire. The emperors passed laws so that craftsmen, lawyers, sewer-cleaners, soldiers, fishermen or teachers were tied to their jobs and land. A son was forced to follow his father's occupation.

6.10 What would the sons of a lawyer and a sewer-cleaner think of these laws?
AT 2.8

Barbarian invasions

Savage tribes approached the Rhine and Danube, driven from their homes thousands of miles away in Asia by the even more savage Huns. The Roman armies could not keep them out. In AD 378 the Visigoths were accepted as allies and allowed to set up their own kingdoms in Gaul and Spain. The Alani, Burgundi, Vandals and Suebi followed them. In AD 408 Alaric the Goth sacked Rome, but moved on to Spain. In AD 429 the Vandals crossed to north Africa. The Romans fought on, and in AD 451, in their last victory, drove Attila and his Huns out of central France.

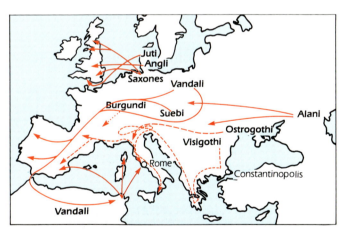

The barbarian invasions of the Roman Empire.

Only four years later the Vandals sailed back from Africa and sacked Rome: half was left in ruins for ever. The aqueducts no longer brought water into the city, and farmers could not supply it with food. Its population sunk to 20,000 – only those who could feed themselves from their gardens and allotments in the former parks.

6.11 What would happen in London if food could not reach the city?
AT 1.3

In AD 475 the last emperor, Romulus Augustulus, was deposed by Odoacer, the mutinous captain of his German mercenary army. Italy became a German kingdom. The Empire of the West was over. At Constantinople the Byzantine Empire, as it is known, lasted for another thousand years, right up to AD 1453. It remained a centre of learning and Greek and Latin literature, law and Christianity. It even survived when the Crusaders sacked it, in anger because they had failed to take Jerusalem. Finally, weak and poor, it was overrun by the Turks. But that is another story.

Britain leaves the empire

The end of Britain as a Roman province had come earlier. The emperor Honorius had to withdraw all the legions from Britain to help defend Italy. The Britons appealed to Honorius in AD 410 for help against Saxon invasions: he could only suggest that they defended themselves. The legions never came back.

Britain after the Romans

Contact with Rome was not lost entirely. Christianity 53 spread both in Britain and on the continent, where most of the barbarians were converted to Christianity. Bede, a British monk, wrote a history of the English Church. He reports a visit by the French bishop Germanus in AD 429 to a British army fighting the Picts:

> **SOURCE 6D**
>
> Germanus declared himself general, and set an ambush. The fierce hordes of the enemy came near, suspecting nothing, sure they were not observed. Three times the priest cried out 'Alleluia', and a shout rang out from our men. The hosts of the enemy were stricken with terror, threw away their swords, and fled, to be drowned in the river behind them.

6.12 We know that St. Germanus did come to Britain: what was Bede's purpose in telling this unlikely story?
AT 2.5

The strong walls of British towns protected the people so long as they were ready to defend them. Life went on, even if luxuries were no longer imported from the continent. At Verulamium, for example, the water supply was still working, well after AD 450.

But by AD 500 the Saxons, Jutes and Angles had arrived and settled to stay. They had no interest in towns, and used Roman roads to mark the bound-aries of their farms. Roman Britain had gone: the England of the Angles was beginning to take its place.

6.13 *What caused the final breakdown of the Roman way of life in Britain?*

The Legacy of Rome – Latin, literature, art and architecture

Modern languages

Life in the Roman empire did not stop just because an emperor was deposed. Law and order disappeared: no one ordered the repair of roads and bridges: there was no one to pay for it. Everyone had to find or grow their own food. But citizens and barbarians lived side by side. As they spoke to each other, common languages developed. The basis was Latin, for this had been spoken everywhere. Latin blended with the languages of the invaders, and became the early forms of Spanish, Portuguese, French, Italian and Romanian: these are called *Romance* languages. In England the language of the original Celtic inhabitants and the German of the invading Saxons were an extra influence. But English contains thousands of words based on Latin: thirty-two different words in this paragraph come from Latin.

6.14 *Alibi, visa, post mortem, et cetera are un-changed Latin words which we still use: what do they mean? Can you find any more?*

Centuries later the empire-builders of Europe took their languages all over the world. Virgil's promise ◁53 had almost come true, as you can see from the map below.

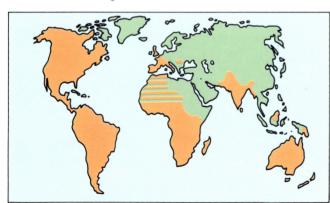

The shaded areas show where Romance languages or English are in the main written or spoken languages, or are used for official and commercial purposes.

Libraries and learning

In hard times Christianity gained strength. Ordinary people looked to their priests for education and learning, law and order.

Monastery libraries collected the surviving books of Greek and Latin, and monks copied them when they wore out. Parchment books were often re-used: the original text was washed off to make way for some Christian writing. But when an interest in learning revived, monasteries and libraries restocked their shelves with new copies of ancient authors.

Knowledge from the past

The ancient civilisations of Egypt, Mesopotamia, and Persia had all added to the knowledge of astronomy, technology, mathematics and archi-tecture. The Hebrews and Greeks had made their contributions in religion, philosophy, politics, literature and art. All this had been absorbed by the Romans, and expanded. Most important, it had all been written down, in Greek or Latin.

Many of these skills were forgotten after the fall of Rome, but in the Renaissance (AD 1300 onwards), men again had time to read and study, to discover what they had lost. To regain these secrets, scholars rescued many important books from old libraries, monastery attics and cathedral outbuildings. Many had disappeared for ever: for example, of the 142 books of Livy's History of Rome, only 35 were found. But by the end of the fifteenth century almost all the Latin and Greek literature we have today was in print. Greek writers created all the main forms of writing – tragedy, comedy, biography, history, poetry, oratory, the scientific treatise and the novel. Latin authors preserved and developed them, then passed them on to us. Without this 'classical' writ-ing, modern history, literature and 'civilisation' would be very different.

Books

To make paper, thin strips from the Egyptian papyrus reed were put side by side in two layers, one vertical, one horizontal. They were glued and pressed together, then smoothed and polished, to make a sheet about 300 mm square. A scribe was given a portion of an author's manuscript, and copied it onto a papyrus sheet with pen and ink (made of resin and soot). The separate sheets were glued together edge to edge, to form a continuous strip, or scroll, up to 10 metres long. An ornamental wooden rod was fitted to one or both ends of the scroll, which was rolled round one rod.

These *volumes*, from the Latin word 'to roll', were then sold by booksellers: they stored them in rows of pigeonholes.

Late in the empire, parchment made from animal skins was used instead of papyrus. Then the square sheets were stitched together at one edge only, so that something much like a modern book was made: this was called a *codex*.

Law and government

For centuries after the fall of Rome, rulers used Roman law to help them keep order in their kingdoms. Many modern legal systems copy its ideas and young lawyers still study them: here are some:

> **SOURCE 6E**
>
> - No man shall be a judge in his own case.
> - A man should have the right to face his accusers.
> - No man can be tried for the same crime twice.
> - No appeal for mercy should be made while a case is being tried.

6.15 Why do you think medieval kings preferred to use Roman laws rather than write their own? `AT 1.3`

But Renaissance men read about more than law. They read about freedom. They saw how the Greeks had been free to question and explore themselves and the world around them. One of the greatest experiments had been government by democracy, in which all the free adult male citizens had a say. (Though women could not vote, or take any official part in government – as was the case in this country until AD 1918 – we know that in matters that concerned them they strictly instructed their husbands how to vote!)

The Roman empire, of course, gave no share in government to the ordinary people. But its writers had written about freedom and democracy. Their ideas about government have shaped our lives ever since. Many modern nations call themselves 'Republics' as the Romans did, many are governed by a 'Senate'. Napoleon called himself 'Emperor' and 'First Consul'. Queen Victoria was also 'Empress of India'. The national emblem of the United States and Germany is the imperial eagle. The Russian Tzar, the German Kaiser and the Shah of Persia have all disappeared: but their titles all came from the word 'Caesar'.

6.16 Make a list of the modern 'republics' and modern 'senates' you can find. `AT 1.2`

Medicine

The Greeks had made wonderful discoveries in medicine and anatomy, but the Romans had more practical experience. Every military camp had its own hospital and medical staff. Roman doctors learnt how to keep soldiers fit in peacetime, and how to heal their wounds in war. Surgeons could amputate successfully, and the different kinds of surgical instruments which have been discovered prove that they could tackle all sorts of minor operations. Vegetius's books on the diseases of mules and cattle also survive: his textbook of military science is still studied in army colleges.

A collection of Roman surgical instruments.

Galen, the court physician of the emperor Marcus Aurelius, wrote about anatomy, physiology, pathology and many other medical subjects. His works remained the standard textbooks in medical schools until the seventeenth century.

Military hospitals were copied in Roman towns, and became models for the hospitals in the Middle Ages. Roman aqueducts and underground sewage systems, hygiene and medical care were unequalled until Victorian times.

6.17 *Why do you think standards of hygiene declined after the end of the empire?.*

AT 1.4

Visible remains

There are Roman remains which we can visit all over Britain. The streets of modern towns are often built over the Roman streets buried beneath them, and preserve the grid pattern the Romans laid down. Modern trunk roads and railways follow the lines of Roman roads. The portrait statues and tombstone carvings produced by Roman artists show real originality, and still bring the ancient people to life.

Roman triumphal arches, like the Arch of Titus in the Roman forum, were imitated by later rulers: the Arc de Triomphe in Paris, and Marble Arch in London are good examples. Medieval craftsmen copied their many-figured friezes on cathedral doorways, as at Wells Cathedral below.

Architecture

The Greeks had put up splendid buildings all round the Mediterranean, with gleaming marble and decorative carvings painted in strong colours. But they were simple buildings, with beams of stone or wood resting on two walls or columns. The Romans were more practical men. Architects learned how to use arches, vaults and domes. Engineers made great cranes so that blocks of stone and barrels of concrete could be hoisted to the top of high buildings. Much larger interior spaces could now be covered. No one improved on Roman building techniques until the Victorians learnt to reinforce concrete with steel rods.

Barates and Regina

Two pieces of evidence finish our story. A tombstone from Tyneside has a Latin inscription meaning:

'To the memory of Barates of Palmyra, army veteran, who lived 68 years.' (Palmyra is an oasis-city in the scorching Syrian desert.)

On another tombstone from nearby South Shields is:

'To the memory of Regina, of the Catuvellaunian tribe, who died aged 30, freedwoman and wife of Barates of Palmyra (who set this up).'

Underneath in Palmyrene script is written:

'Regina, freedwoman of Barates. Alas!'

Regina wears a necklace and bracelets. In one hand she has a distaff and spindle; with the other she is holding up the lid of a casket with a large keyhole, in which she kept her jewels. By her left foot is her workbasket, with her balls of wool.

After leaving the army Barates became a successful trader, bought a slave girl, became fond of her, freed her and married her. How sad is that one lonely line of his native language, which only Barates can have understood!

A soldier from a Syrian oasis, and a slave girl of Belgic descent from East Anglia, buried in the north of England near a wall designed by an emperor of Rome who was born in Spain. This is a strange mixture of different races and beliefs, but it was typical of the Roman empire. It was also largely why it was so vigorous and lasted so long.

Index

This index lists the most important subjects, names and places in the book, and the pages on which they occur. It contains all the ancient authors whose writings are quoted. You will also find some other subjects, which are not mentioned here, listed on the Contents page, page (ii).

Acknowledgements

The authors and publisher are grateful to the following for permission to reproduce photographs:

The Ancient Art and Architecture Collection/Ronald Sheridan's Photo Library: Pages 1 (top), 5, 18 (right), 19 (bottom), 24 (right), 25, 26 (top and bottom), 32 (top), 35 (left), 36 (centre), 38 (bottom), 40 (bottom), 41, 42 (bottom left and right), 44 (bottom), 47 (top), 49 (top right), 54 (bottom), 61, 62 (top), 64 (bottom) ● J. Badcock: Pages 3 (both), 4 (right), 7 (bottom), 20 (right), 45 (bottom) ● Barnaby's Picture Library: Page 59 (top) Bill Meadows ● Bridgeman Art Library/ Museo a Gallerie Nazionale di Capodimonte, Naples: Page 31 ● Cambridge University Collection, copyright reserved: Page 68 (bottom); reproduced with the permission of the Controller of HMSO: Pages 63 (top), 65 (bottom) ● Peter Clayton: Pages 26 (centre), 27 (right), 30 (bottom right), 38 (top), 56, 64 (top), 74 (bottom) ● Colchester Archaeological Trust Ltd: Page 63 (bottom) ● Colchester Museums: Page 58 (right) ● C.M. Dixon: Pages 6 (both), 7 (top), 8 (top, bottom right), 9 (bottom left and right), 11, 14, 35 (top right), 38 (centre both), 48, 49 (top left), 50 (bottom) ● English Heritage: Page 57 ● Werner Forman Archive: Pages 39, 42 (top) ● Grosvenor Museum, Chester: Pages 16, 62 (bottom) ● Sonia Halliday: Pages 8 (bottom left), 44 (top), 54 (top) L. Lushington ● Robert Harding Picture Library: Pages 34 (bottom), 46 (top), 49 (bottom) ● Michael Holford: Pages 1 (bottom), 15 (top), 20 (left), 38 (right), 50 (top), 69, 73 ● Mansell Collection/Alinari: Pages 4 (left), 10 (both), 12 (right), 15 (bottom), 17 (top), 18 (left), 32 (top), 37, 43, 51 ● Scala, Italy: Pages 29 (top), 46 (bottom), 53 (top) ● Society of Antiquaries, London: Page 58 (left) ● Graham Tingay: Page 74 (top) ● University of Cambridge School Classics Project: Pages 28 (left), 32 (bottom left and right), 40 (top) ● Westair Photography: Page 70.

Every effort has been made to contact copyright holders and we apologise if any have been overlooked.

First published in 1991 by:
Stanley Thornes (Publishers) Ltd
Old Station Drive
Leckhampton
CHELTENHAM GL53 0DN
England

British Library Cataloguing in Publication Data

Tingay, Graham
    The Romans and their Empire. — (History matters)
    I. Title   II. Badcock, John   III. Series
    937

    ISBN 0–7487–1186–4

Typeset by Tech-Set, Gateshead, Tyne & Wear.
Printed and bound in Hong Kong.